Advanced Praise f
Awakening With Sanskrit

"In the realms of merging Eastern mystical technology and practical method, Dr. Katy Jane is one of the planet's most valuable teachers. *Awakening with Sanskrit* is a small yet intelligent and practical book for beginning to work with the vast complexity of Sanskrit. Dr. Katy seamlessly makes this ancient and often esoteric approach to meditation completely accessible to the modern practitioner—and in the process, allows it to become more real to us. This is a book I will recommend to all of the students who work in my Ayurveda and Tantrik yoga programs."

— Katie Silcox, *New York Times* bestselling author of
Healthy, Happy, Sexy: Ayurveda Wisdom for Modern Women

"*Awakening with Sanskrit* is a refined (*samskrta*) reflection of the highly elaborated language that is the subject of this fascinating book. Dr. Katy Jane knowledgeably and passionately explains that Sanskrit is a living technology that can lead people to higher states of consciousness and equanimity. Drawing from decades of studying and teaching—in America and India, in Western universities and traditional guru/student relationships, in person and via online platforms—Dr. Katy reveals that reciting the sounds of Sanskrit is an integral part of yoga practice. Reading this book in conjunction with using her series of learning products will add so much to everyone's quest for growth, healing, and awakening."

— Dr. Marcy Braverman Goldstein, Sanskrit scholar and creator of
Sanskrit Revolution

"Dr. Katy Jane has brought to life the language of the divine beings. This book is inspirational and contagious; it invites one to move from sound towards silence. The reader might experience the presence of divine fragrance and the dance of *shakti* while going through this beautiful pilgrimage that the book promises."

— Indu Arora, Author of
Yoga: Ancient Heritage Tomorrow's Vision* and *Mudra: The Sacred Secret

"Dr. Katy Jane's book is an insightful, personal, and inspiring foray into the majesty of the Sanskrit language. Combining stories from her life's journey with esoteric teachings of the yoga tradition, she skillfully outlines a path of transformation through sacred sound that anyone can take. New and experienced yoga practitioners will find a captivating story as well as practical tools to deepen personal understanding through direct experience. I whole-heartedly recommend this book to anyone hoping to expand their consciousness and connect to their essential Self."

— Christina Sell, author of
***Yoga From the Inside Out: Making Peace with Your Body Through Yoga*,**
***My Body is a Temple: Yoga as a Path to Wholeness*, and**
A Deeper Yoga: Beyond Image to Wholeness and Freedom

Awakening *with* Sanskrit

Introduction to the Sacred Language of Yoga

DR. KATY JANE

Dedication

For all the great seers, the rishis, whose extraordinary realization enhanced the world with the art and science of the Vedas in Sanskrit. And for all my teachers, their teachers, and all who taught before them who kept the knowledge of the seers unbroken for centuries so that all yogis can partake in its splendor.

Original Sanskrit translations: Katy Jane, Ph.D.
Cover & eBook design: Bigger Fish Studios

White Swan Press

First Edition Printing: August, 2019
Printed in the USA

For additio
nal information send email or visit online locations:

- www.DrKatyJane.com
- www.SanskritforYogis.com
- namaste@drkatyjane.com

Contents

Dr. Katy Jane

About Dr. Katy Jane

Named one of the "Top 75 Yogis Who Are Shifting the Planet" by *Origin*, Dr. Katy Jane is a Sanskrit and Vedic scholar, spiritual facilitator, and author. Her guiding vision is rooted in the ancient Veda of India—a system of transformational wisdom—that's at the heart of enlightened living. Its aim is to advance the human soul toward greater happiness and fulfillment and is available to everyone regardless of culture, religion or beliefs. It is *sanatana dharma*, the eternal way of universal truth.

While earning her doctorate in Religious Studies from the University of California, Santa Barbara, Katy spent five years studying Vedic Sanskrit under the guidance of traditional *pandits*. With the boon of American Institute of Indian Studies and Ford Foundation grants, Katy studied the Sanskrit, Hindi and Bengali languages in Calcutta as a scholar-in-residence at the Ramakrishna Institute of Culture. With the aid of Fulbright-Hayes and University of California Presidential grants for her doctoral research, she traveled the length and breadth of India recording the life stories and teachings of yogis, saints and religious adepts to gain insight into Hindu concepts and methods of spiritual enlightenment.

Upon completing her degree, she served as an assistant professor of world religions and Sanskrit at Simpson College, California Polytechnic University, the University of Colorado and Naropa University before stepping in to fill a gap in the growing western yoga community. Few yoga teachers were including Sanskrit in their yoga teaching and practice as it was traditionally embraced in its Indian context.

To offer sincere yoga teachers and students access to the traditional Vedic approach to learning Sanskrit, Dr. Katy created *Sanskrit for Yogis* in 2006. Her goal was to provide non-academic beginners an easy—and yet profoundly transformative—introduction to Sanskrit as a technology of consciousness, and not a "dead" academic language.

For over a decade, Katy's shared the Vedic method of learning Sanskrit to many aspiring yoga teachers and students worldwide through live and online trainings. Today she resides in the Himalayas of India where she serves as director of yoga studies at Dunagiri Retreat and where she leads in-depth immersions in traditional Vedic Sanskrit, women's kriya yoga and meditation. As an expert Vedic astrologer, she also serves as a life insight advisor, offering personal consultations based on the ancient art and science of *Jyotisha* (Vedic Astrology).

Forward

"And your disciple's disciple will be responsible for the spread of yoga to the west,"
~ Mahavatar Babaji

It's been over 30 years since a fatal choice changed my life—a choice that ignited my quest for truth and resulted in the discoveries about Sanskrit you're about to read.

It began with a knock on my door. "Are you ready, Katy?" my friend Danny asked, poking his curly head in through the screen door to see if I was all set to go. The car was running. I was prepared to jump in.

It was the last day of summer break before my senior year in high school. Days were already getting shorter and this was one last chance to feel the freedom of no school, of being just 16, and of taking risks you can only take when you're young.

What happened next, to this day I cannot explain. I said, "No."

Every part of me wanted to go. I didn't want to miss the party and the kids I'd meet there. But I said, "No." And Danny and our other friend drove off without me.

The following morning, I awoke to yet another knock on the door. This time it was a police officer asking me if I knew the names of my friends (the ones who were last reported to have been at my house). When I confirmed I knew them, the officer gave the solemn news that they'd died along with five other classmates in a drunk driving accident. They'd all been drinking from a stolen keg of beer and later collided into each other. All died instantly.

Later when I surveyed the wreckage, I saw the seat I should have occupied. It was crumpled. I should have been crumpled. In a split second, I made a decision that saved my life. But in the space of a single thought, I could have been dead along with my seven friends.

It was that random. And because of its randomness, I became obsessed with questioning, "Why?"

I lost all interest in life except for "why." I didn't see the point in being born only to die. "Why me and not the others?" "Why the others and not me?" These thoughts circled round and round in my mind, making me appear morose. My mood, in particular, caught the attention of my high school English teacher.

"Here, I think you should read this," he said, approaching me one day in the school hallway. Then he handed me a copy of Paramahansa Yogananada's *Autobiography of a Yogi* and—just like that—changed my fate. In the same split second in which I could have died, the answer I was seeking was given to me. It was yoga.

I had little idea of what yoga was. But I was going to have it. I started taking yoga classes wherever I could find them. The way of breathing and chanting I was learning expanded my awareness toward something far greater than my limited thinking. Something was waking up in me. Mostly, yoga was helping me to heal my grief and seek answers from within myself instead of through outside validation.

Although I studied with many masterful teachers at that time, I was irresistibly drawn to an elusive character featured prominently in "the Book," Mahavatar Babaji. He's said to be an immortal yogi who dwells in the Himalayas—yet appears at random to his disciples when they need his guidance. I wondered if it was he who'd saved me from the fatal car crash—because the voice I followed certainly could not have been my own. And I wondered if it was Babaji who'd appeared the night before I was born to my mother.

My mother always told me a strange bedtime story—the story of her one and only mystical experience. Although she never explained why, she was terrified of losing me in childbirth. The night before my birth, she lay in bed frozen in a tight grip of fear. Then she explained, "The room at once filled with light and a being stood before me with long black hair and beard, robed in white. I will never forget his eyes. They were so beautiful and full of sublime love. All my fear melted away and since that day I've never felt afraid again."

Mahavatar Babaji

The being communicated via his eyes, telepathically, to my mother. He showed her my birth and reassured her that she would have a healthy daughter. "I always thought he might have been Jesus," Mom—a confirmed agnostic—would remark. "He had that Christlike energy."

Yogananda described Babaji similarly in his autobiography. Even though I believed the immortal yogi is a being who transcends the physical, I developed a longing to meet Babaji in the same way a previous disciple, Lahiri Mahasaya, had encountered him in 1862—on foot, in the Himalayas.

Lahiri Mahasaya had been working for the Indian railways under British rule when he'd been mysteriously transferred to a remote outpost, the army cantonment town of Ranikhet in the eastern Himalayan foothills. Fond of trekking in forests, Lahiri found himself in a veritable mountain paradise with miles of oak and rhododendron spread out in rolling hills.

The irresistible landscape beckoned him out for a trek one day. With no plan of where he was going, he traced his steps along the River Gagas until he reached its source in a village called Dunagiri. There he was lured by a primeval forest to continue his trek deeper into the wilderness that surrounds this sweet hamlet.

Suddenly among the chirping birds and insects, he heard his name being called. "Lahiri, Lahiri!" Startled, he turned to face a beautiful being—a forest yogi, whose physique shone with an almost supernatural glow that came from within. That yogi seemed to know him. He seemed to be expecting him.

"Come, your cave is waiting for you," the copper-haired ascetic announced. Then he led Lahiri toward the opening of a dark cavern and invited him to sit inside. Lahiri recognized that he'd been there before, and this was his Guru from a previous birth.

Reunited in the cave, Babaji initiated his disciple in *kriya yoga*, a path leading toward advanced states of human consciousness and spiritual emancipation. For the first time in history, yoga was no longer a practice reserved for world-denying monks. Anyone could benefit from yoga. Yoga became India's gift to humanity in that one meeting. "And your disciple's disciple will be responsible for the spread of yoga to the west," Babaji foretold.

Indeed, it came to pass. Lahiri's disciple, Sri Yukteshwar, had a famous student—Paramahansa Yogananda—who's credited with transplanting yoga to the other side of the world. And his book landed in my hands (as it has in millions of hands worldwide in all languages) at a crucial moment. It began my search.

Because of *Autobiography of a Yogi*, I developed an insatiable thirst to meet Babaji in a Himalayan forest myself. Not knowing much about that region of the world, I equated the Himalayas with Nepal and thus began my search for him there. This—as you'll read in the little book that follows—is how I discovered Sanskrit.

My journey to Nepal as a teenager resulted in my decision to pursue Religious Studies and Sanskrit and eventually earn my doctorate in both. It brought me to my first gurus who initiated my lifelong practice of yoga and meditation. It inspired my inquiry into yoga philosophy, Vedic Sanskrit and world religions. It led me to teach Sanskrit as a *sadhana* (spiritual discipline) to many sincere yogis. And it's led me to the Mother from whom I'm learning about devotion. In a split second—in the space it took to say "no" to death and "yes" to life— my entire path was laid out.

Yet somehow in all this I'd forgotten about Babaji. I'd forgotten how I roamed the deep forests of Nepal's Himalayas looking for him. I'd forgotten how I'd searched the face of every *sadhu* and yogi I'd encountered to see if they were the "one" I was drawn to. I'd forgotten how I longed for that connection I felt to be validated by him calling *my* name.

Then it was 2010. I hadn't been back to India in a decade. I was caught up in serving as an assistant professor of world religions, teaching Sanskrit classes in many yoga trainings and keeping up with a growing Vedic astrology consultation practice. I didn't realize it, but I had lost my way. The spark had gone out. Every bit of me was going out toward everything external—giving all my energy along with it. And nothing was coming back in.

When I finally realized I was burned out, my then-husband and I decided to get out of town and drove from Boulder, Colorado to Sedona, Arizona—a well-known vortex. There in the midst of that powerful desert energy, I had a dream. In it, my first guru was calling me back. "Come back to India this year," he said plaintively. "It's time."

I knew I had to return.

Haunted by my guru's instruction, I planned a trip that May to attend the annual *chardham yatra*—the pilgrimage to Hinduism's four holiest shrines. Ten eager yoga teachers joined me and off we went in a small minibus through the broken and precarious narrow roads of Garwahl, the western foothills of the Himalayas.

I was an inexperienced tour guide. The drive was long and treacherous. And somehow since the last time I'd been in India till then, everyone suddenly owned a car. Throngs of pilgrims crowded every nook and cranny of what once a remote wilderness was. I regretted my decision to undertake such a foolish journey in the dead heat of May and vowed never to return to India again.

Then I met someone who'd lived my parallel life in India—on Facebook of all places—and I was pulled back.

One of the pilgrims posted photos on social media. Those photos caught the eye of someone online. That someone was Piyush Kumar who'd just completed work on his Dunagiri Retreat in the eastern Himalayan foothills and who was searching for yogis he thought might like to visit such a place.

Gangotri, the source of the Ganges River.

Badrinath Temple, one of the four most holy pilgrimage sites.

Pilgrims at the Ganges River, Rishikesh.

Lady taking holy dip in the Ganges.

It was such a chance meeting like every major turn on my journey. In the split second it took for Piyush to leave a cryptic comment on one of the photos, my life took a radical change.

We'd exchanged messages in response to that comment in which I learned that Dunagiri is the home of an ancient goddess temple dedicated to Vaishnavi Ma, considered a "seat of power." And he mentioned something else. "The cave is here," he wrote as if I knew.

I hurriedly entered his website address and there he was—Babaji—front and center on the home page along with a photo of *the cave* where the fateful meeting between Lahiri and Babaji took place. Suddenly my life came full circle. I made immediate plans to visit Dunagiri.

Babaji's Cave at Dunagiri.

The moment my feet touched down in this mountain paradise surrounding the cave, I knew my destiny was somehow complete. What I had once sought was now seeking me. I returned to the original inspiration of my search and just as I'd found Sanskrit in Nepal, Sanskrit again found me in Dunagiri.

Dunagiri is just opposite a Himalayan meadow— locally called *Baidini Bugyal*—which is said to be where the rishis originally cognized the Vedas. (*Baidini* is the local dialect version of *vaidini*, meaning "belonging to the Vedas," and a *bugyal* is a Himalayan high plateau.)

As I stepped down from the bus we'd chartered, I heard the Vedas being chanted in Sanskrit loud and clear. I thought Piyush had called a group of priests to welcome us with Sanskrit chanting. But it was late at night and everyone was fast asleep. I heard it in the air.

There's something about the elevation combined with the quality of air in the presence of soaring snow-peaked mountains that brings a unique clarity of mind, which is fit to see beyond its ordinary habits of thought. Silence shrieks loudly in such a place. It shuts out all the other noise. And you can hear the underlying pulse that often sounds like rhythmic chanting. In the Vedas, this is called *rtambara*, "sound waves of consciousness."

The experience of being so close to the site of Vedic cognition has reignited my love of Sanskrit and deepened my commitment to the journey I began so long ago. It's now been over a decade since I originally published *Awakening with Sanskrit*. While the content hasn't changed much since then, the author certainly has. My journey brought me back to where it all began and reinvigorated my path, like a holy dip in the Ganges River.

Not only my soul—but its expression in my Sanskrit teaching—has received a renewal. And so, I present the latest version of *Awakening with Sanskrit*. May it inspire you on your own path and join me as all my Sanskrit for Yogis programs experience their rebirth.

Lokah samastha sukhino bhavantu!
May all beings be happy!

Dr. Katy Jane
Dunagiri, India

The beautiful Himalayas high atop Dunagiri Retreat.

A Note on Sanskrit Transliteration

For the ease of comprehension for beginning students of Sanskrit, I have deliberately not employed the conventional academic transliteration of Sanskrit words (IAST: International Alphabet of Sanskrit Transliteration) to avoid confusing English readers. Instead, I've adopted a more colloquial rendering of such terms.

Introduction

My Discovery of Sanskrit

"Every day children sat under the spreading branches of an ancient banyan tree and recited the Vedic texts after their teacher."

~ from the Kena Upanisad

Young student reciting the Veda.

My mouth hung agape. Could someone actually lift off the ground and defy gravity? I couldn't imagine not eating for a single day, let alone for 50 years as the lady saint I was reading about had accomplished. And was it really possible to make oneself invisible?

By the time I'd finished the final chapter of Paramahansa Yogananda's *Autobiography of a Yogi*, I'd discovered a way of enlightenment through self-mastery—yoga—that meant much more than these outward attainments. It showed me I could be more than my limitations. Freedom from suffering was not only possible, it was available—even to me, a troubled teenage girl from a small town in Massachusetts.

Yogananda's stories of yogis and saints who'd attained heightened states of consciousness and miraculous abilities through yoga and meditation inspired me out of my teenage depression. I wanted what they had. I knew there is something more incredible in this life that was beckoning me.

Having awakened to that "something more incredible" at the tender age of sixteen with a near-death experience, I didn't take much at face value. By the time I'd entered college, the thought of earning a degree to get a job and live an unexamined life terrified me.

I made a bold decision to do something different. My plan was to drop out of school, save enough money for a plane ticket and six months of living expenses by waitressing tables, and travel alone to Nepal—where I believed I'd find Babaji, the yogi of yogis.

My intention was so singular, like a burning flame, that I couldn't hear any of the protests coming from my worried mother. "Just where do you think you're going, young lady, to find this so-called *goo-roo*?" She questioned me relentlessly and even attempted to stop me on the way out the door, grabbing hold of the straps of my backpack to pull me back.

My father, on the other hand, just opened the atlas and landed his finger somewhere next to Mumbai. "No, Dad, it's further north. Here's the capital city of Nepal, Kathmandu," I explained as I guided his gaze up toward my beloved Himalayas. "That's where I'm going," I quipped as if every teenager in America was heading there as the new hip hangout. It was 1988 and globalization was still in its infancy. Nepal, to my father, may as well have been the moon and I was trying to make it seem more normal.

Nothing anyone could say, however, dissuaded me from my resolve. I didn't care that it was dangerous to travel alone. I wasn't worried about being a young girl and vulnerable. I knew what I wanted and if I died searching for it, I could at least feel I lived without regrets. College could wait.

As I boarded the plane bound for Kathmandu, I made a promise to myself: *I won't return until I've found it.*

Arriving in Nepal, the plane circled the city as barefoot peasants shooed some errant cows off the runway and finally came in to land. Out of the airport gates, I stepped toward my destiny. I also happened to step in a pile of dung, slipping and falling to the ground. A crowd gathered and laughed unashamedly at my predicament.

Now I understand why. Here was a silly young girl, wielding an oversized backpack, so intent on getting somewhere that she couldn't be bothered to look where she stepped. A kind-looking gentleman offered me his hand.

"Welcome to Nepal," he said brightly. "Why are you here?"

When I told him my plan, he gave me the same incredulous look my family had worn. "What is there in enlightenment?" he questioned. "You're an American. You have everything. There is nothing for you in Nepal!"

Then handing me a card, he concluded, "Call these people. They can help you."

As soon as I arrived at my guesthouse, I read the card's inscription: *United States Peace Corps: Nepali Language Immersions.* The helpful stranger gave me a tip that I hadn't even considered. If I were to meet an enlightened yogi, speaking the native language could prove indispensable. I promptly enrolled.

Following a week of Nepali classes and a barrage of personal questions (which in any other context would seem intrusive and nosey) my teacher, Shankar Narayan, ordered me to gather my things. It was very unusual—and quite improper—for Nepalis to see a young woman traveling by herself and staying alone. I learned this the day before when I shared that I was interned at the Hotel Shiva—a reputed dump of a place housing a coterie of ex-patriots who'd left America during the Nixon administration, hippies with dirty feet, and an obstinate population of bed bugs. Shankar turned pale at my confession and gasped, "Oh, no! That's not a place for a lady to stay."

Immediately following my tutorial, Shankar Narayan hailed a taxi, hauled my bags down the stairs of the Hotel Shiva and gestured for me to get in the back. I had no idea where he was taking me.

We bumped along the narrow streets of Kathmandu, dodging stray cattle, erratic bicyclists, and kids playing crude games of cricket. Then the road opened out of the city toward the village Balaju. I drank in the beauty of purple morning glories set against emerald rice paddies. My eyes met the sweet glance of water buffalos as they waded up to their floppy ears in irrigation canals. I admired the grace of women working in the paddies, swaying in their red saris like a dance. And I swooned at the scent of incense wafting from a small roadside shrine next to an ancient tree.

I thought I'd entered some form of paradise that the rest of the world had lost in its pursuit of "progress." I remembered the small suburban town in which I'd grown up, in contrast, where no one was ever home, where lawns were mowed with gas machines, and where the only form of animal life was securely fastened to a leash and taken out to politely relieve itself twice a day on the carefully manicured grass. For the first time in my life, I felt I'd arrived home thousands of miles from where I'd grown up.

No sooner had that feeling entered my heart, than the taxi stopped at a three-storied cement building. As we approached the entrance, a newborn calf ran out the front door toward its mother in the courtyard. Shankar Narayan nodded to me remarking, "An auspicious sign for you." A man resembling an older, grayer version of Shankar, welcomed us with palms together: *Namaste*.

"Uncle, I've brought an American student to live with you," Shankar announced plaintively.

"Good, good," was all the man said. "Please come."

Over a tin cup of steaming milk tea, I learned that Shankar Narayan's uncle was the head priest of the most sacred Hindu temple in Kathmandu. Whole-heartedly invited to stay as long as I wanted, I was instantly treated like a long-lost daughter. Never in my life had I experienced so much love given by complete strangers to a complete stranger. The Nepali hospitality heaped on me by Krishna Narayan and his family changed me forever.

Offered a room to myself on the first floor of the home, a place of honor next to the family shrine room, every morning at 4:00 a.m. a loud cacophony of strange and rhythmic sounds awakened me. These beautiful, hypnotic and nonsensical melodies put my mind at rest. My breathing became deep and full.

I relaxed totally into the pleasant pulse of warm electricity coursing through my body. Letting go, I forgot the time. Not quite asleep and not quite awake, I entered a natural state of meditation.

My biorhythms quickly adjusted to this morning routine. I found it easy to awake much earlier than I was accustomed, eager to experience the "music" again and again. As soon as Krishna Uncle and his little boy, Babu, had settled in the shrine room, I'd sneak over to the side of the doorway and seat myself in full lotus posture. As their voices grew stronger, faster, and yet precisely rhythmic, I'd dissolve into the sweet sensations that led me to a vast open space within. It felt pure there. I experienced a wakeful awareness that contained no thought. The best way I found to express it was through a blissful smile spread across my face.

"You like our *adhyayanam*?" Krishna Uncle asked me one morning.

Is that what this is called? I wondered to myself. *Adhyaa-yaa-num?*

"I don't know," I answered. "I've never heard this before."

"It is teacher-disciple method," he explained. "I sit. You sit. I chant. You listen. You repeat."

And that's what I did for many, many mornings before I ever learned that I was chanting in Sanskrit. All I knew was that these pure impulses of sound were what energized, enlivened, and awakened my yoga and meditation practice. After chanting, I became so acutely aware of the structures of my subtle body (*marmas, nadis, and cakras*) that pulsed with renewed *prana* (subtle life-force). Spontaneously, my body formed the shapes of the Yoga *asanas*. And my mind and emotions became silent and still.

Once Krishna Uncle was in a very revealing mood. We were sitting together on the roof of his house on low jute stools. It was kite-flying season in Kathmandu and the sky was full of flourish. For many months, I'd asked him about enlightenment to no avail. He'd never answer a single one of my questions. He'd just shake his head slightly side to side with his eyes cast up, as if I'd asked something very good, as if the question alone was sufficient. But that day on the roof, Krishna Uncle felt like talking.

"You know Sanskrit is not a language," he explained. "It is the very mind of God. This world is the spoken breath of God. Our breath is the breath of God. When we direct it back to the divine source with our holy chants, we merge with Him."

I nodded in agreement. Krishna Uncle's words perfectly described what I experienced as I first heard and felt the sounds of Sanskrit. "Is Sanskrit the secret behind enlightenment?" I queried sincerely.

"Yes, correct." Krishna Uncle responded. "You become very intelligent by intoning these sounds. Your mind becomes very clear and open. Your heart becomes happy. The family relations improve. And your life's duty is easily fulfilled."

I knew I'd discovered the secret behind yoga's power to achieve higher states of consciousness and enlightenment. I decided then and there I would dedicate myself to perfecting the art of Vedic chanting in Sanskrit to open myself more to this sweet experience of awakening.

Then one day, Krishna Uncle approached me with a look of concern. "You are not educated," he remarked. "Who will respect you?"

I became confused. *Respect? Why did that matter to me?*

Yet Krishna Uncle persisted in his worry. Finally, he spoke directly. "You must finish your education. It is essential."

"But the only thing I want to learn is what I'm learning here," I argued.

"You can earn your degree in Sanskrit studies," he reasoned. "Then you will be found credible."

After several weeks going back and forth like this, I finally conceded. I'd return to the United States to pursue my studies in Sanskrit. Keeping my word, I enrolled in the Sanskrit program offered through the Department of Religious Studies at the University of California, Santa Barbara.

Initially there were 25 students in my academic Sanskrit class, which even on the first day was brutally difficult. It reminded me of the day my father taught me to ski—by pushing me down the hill! Nothing about the way Sanskrit was taught in the university remotely resembled my shrine room lessons at Krishna Uncle's home. I felt like I accidently walked in on a theoretical physics class that demanded rigorous understanding of calculus as a pre-requisite. I checked my schedule. No, this was the right room. And this was Sanskrit class.

On the second day of class, only five students showed up. By the third day, attendance had dwindled to just three of us. The only reason I remained was because my teacher, Mrs. Nandini Iyer, pulled me aside whispering, "Only those with good past-life merit are able to learn Sanskrit." She stoked my fire. I certainly was going to be one of those with good past-life merit!

The grammatical structure of Sanskrit is so intricate, complex and difficult, it's a miracle that I had the dedication and discipline to stick it out for five years. In fact, I performed well enough in my studies to be accepted into the masters and doctorate program in the Department of Religious Studies at the University of California, Santa Barbara.

Yet I longed to experience Sanskrit as it had been orally transmitted from teacher to student for thousands of years. Although I had gained proficiency in grammar and translation, I felt that the sacred status and enlightening power of Sanskrit had been totally lost by the academic, "dead classical language" approach. I wanted to immerse myself in the oral transmission of the sacred language from teacher to student as I had in Nepal and re-enliven it in my spiritual practice.

At that point, I'd studied hard, labored in my understanding of grammar and syntax, and memorized multitudes of complex rules, paradigms, and declensions. I was quite confident I was going to become a great Sanskrit and yoga master! Fortunately, I received a grant to return to India for five years to study with traditional Sanskrit teachers. Receiving the grant was relatively easy. Finding a teacher who'd accept a non-Brahmin, unmarried, American woman as a student was another matter.

I sent out over a hundred letters to potential teachers and not one was answered. I understood that it was uncustomary for a Brahmin male master of Sanskrit to impart the sacred transmission of Vedic chanting to an American woman. Krishna Uncle had made a great exception by teaching me, which I hadn't fully appreciated at the time. For all other traditional teachers, it appeared, I simply did not fulfill the purity and caste requirements that forbid anyone but a Brahmin male to chant the auspicious Vedas in Sanskrit.

I almost gave up in despair when a letter arrived from India. It was addressed to me by a Sanskrit *pandita* (scholar), Abhijit Chattopadyay, who informed me that he wasn't interested at first in accepting me as a student. But then he had two dreams that convinced him otherwise. In the first dream, his teacher appeared to him telling him that if this knowledge had been kept in the hands of women it would never be lost! And in the second dream, he envisioned a foreign woman teaching many women students of yoga Vedic chanting in Sanskrit. In his letter, he described them as "oceans of ladies." So I'd passed the first test and found a suitable teacher. And I was on my way to Calcutta to begin my Vedic Sanskrit studies.

After 36 grueling hours on the "Mail Express" train from Bangalore, I arrived in Calcutta's Howrah Station, feeling immediately that I'd met my match of what I thought up to then I could tolerate in India. Exiting the train, I was pulled forcibly into a stream of people that became a river and eventually an ocean. It carried me swiftly across Howrah Bridge over the Ganges River, called here the Hooghly. A leper offered his hand and I seized it, forgetting my instinct to recoil. It was all I could do to keep from drowning in that sea of people.

This was my introduction to the goddess of humanity herself, Kali, who abides in Calcutta as her little finger—and on whom we all hang, as we did as children on our own mothers to keep from getting lost.

It's said that India is sacred because it's the actual body of the mother goddess of creation, Sati, and whose body parts "sit" in various places. In Calcutta, her little finger alone resides. It's such a small digit, such a small unit of time. She is time herself—that tiny, split-second instant that changes everything.

For me coming to Calcutta was that split-second timing I'd grown accustomed to as a signal that my life was on track. I never planned nor desired to go to that city, let alone live there for two years. Frankly, the place terrified me. I'd only heard of the beggars and the insufferable heat. I had no idea how magnificent the Mother's little finger is!

At the last minute I'd received my teacher's letter. And even he recovered my original letter from the dust bin on a sudden change of mind! So, there I was in Calcutta and she had a lot to teach me.

Somehow from out of that great sea of humanity, I managed to locate the taxi waiting to take me to the Ramakrishna Mission where I was invited as a "scholar in residence." But as it was still early morning, the driver was busy in prayer—ringing a bell, waving an incense stick and muttering in a melodious low tone.

Before him on the dashboard stood a tiny icon of Kali—the object of his worship. Her hair was in a wild array, framing her entire naked body from head to foot. Donning a garland of skulls and skirt of cutoff arms, fangs jutted out from each side of her mouth. She was sticking her tongue out at me, which I was always told was rude, but in her case showed her invincible, "I don't care what you think," attitude. She was both extremely frightening and somehow extremely loveable. I didn't know if I should laugh or cry seeing her standing triumphant on the corpse of her husband, holding up the head of her enemy as a trophy.

I shuddered knowing somehow my ego was next.

Then the driver, noting my fascination with his miniature goddess, said matter-of-factly, "She is our Mother." How could that frightening demoness be anyone's mother? And yet, she became mine.

I've recently learned the way fetuses develop in the womb. Your hand, for example, is created because all the unnecessary cells around what will become your fingers and thumb die off. What begins as an undeveloped stump turns into your beautiful hand through death. The same thing happened to me in Calcutta. Kali mothered me by making me die to all the concepts I'd learned up until then.

Soon after my arrival in Calcutta, I followed the cryptic instructions my would-be Sanskrit teacher gave me to reach his home. I first navigated the bus that gave me a swift and exciting tour of what felt more like a dance floor than city streets. Everyone—car, animal, bicycle and pedestrian—was moving in and out of the traffic, to a timed rhythm. Finally, the bus stopped at an intersection where no cars could go. Then I boarded a cycle rickshaw, whose driver pedaled me through delightful sweet lanes snaking among Bengali-style homes with thatched roofs and cows tied up out front. Had I not known I was in a major metropolis, I would have sworn I was in a village.

On foot I followed an even smaller lane next to a jackfruit tree as the instructions directed until I came to a tiny whitewashed cottage with a small pond full of teeming fish in front. My teacher's mother—a widow—greeted me at the gate, a vision in pure white from her hair, to her sari, to the glow around her. I smelled the incense wafting out from inside. This was a brahmin's home.

When I first met my teacher, he didn't seem very impressed with me. In fact, for two weeks he mostly ignored me. I'd come for my daily lesson and sit in the tiny drawing room outside the family puja room. Plate after plate of Bengali sweets were presented to me. I delighted in *rosgulla* and *sandesh*, but not a word of Sanskrit was uttered, nor any mention of when my lessons might begin.

Airmail letter from Calcutta.

With Vedanta teacher, Mrs. Babani Ganguli (far left) and her Auntie in Calcutta.

Dr. Katy with her Guru's Ma in Calcutta.

Kali Puja celebration, Calcutta.

Finally after several weeks, Panditji asked if I'd recite a simple line in Sanskrit. I thought, "This is so easy. I'm really going to make great progress. I can translate this. I can tell all the different parts of speech and analyze the grammar." With confidence, I pronounced the first word.

The sound had barely escaped my lips when my teacher blocked his ears and said, "Oh, this is terrible! It's the worst Sanskrit I've ever heard in my life! You must start at the beginning."

The Author as a young Sanskrit student in Calcutta, 1992.

I thought, "*What does he mean? How can he not be impressed with me? I've spent so much time studying Sanskrit. Surely, I'm no beginner!*"

But beginner I became. For more than six months I was only permitted to chant the 50 syllables of the Sanskrit alphabet every day and nothing more advanced. I thought I'd go insane. The repetition for eight hours or more per day was maddening. Just when I thought I'd perfected a sound, Panditji would clap his hands and make me repeat it again and again, each time discovering a new flaw.

In India, it's traditional that teachers don't tell you the reason why you're given certain tasks. If you ask why, you'll be told, "Yes, you will chant." And then if you ask again, "But why do I have to chant the same sounds over and over again, every day for months and months?" My teacher always answered simply, "You will chant it. No problem."

I was so discouraged, humiliated, and full of despair. According to tradition, you can't just dump your teacher because you don't like his or her method. You have to persevere. You have to give up your ego in order to make any kind of progress in yoga and meditation. As a student you must realize that you're not in charge.

Indians seem to naturally understand the *guru*-disciple relationship. Children are often asked, "If god or *guru* should stand before you, whose feet do you touch first?" The answer is obvious—the *guru's* because she brought you to god.

Once when I was in India, I met an accomplished yogi outside a temple in Rudraprayag. He asked me why I'd come to India and I explained that I'd brought a group of yoga teachers to experience her sacred culture on pilgrimage. He responded mockingly, "No one in America knows what a true yogi is."

I started to feel offended when he explained, "It's not about the poses, but the depth of your surrender." He shared further. "When I was learning yoga my *guru* only permitted me to perform one yoga *asana* and that was *tadasana* ("mountain pose")! I practiced it—and only it—every day for 12 years."

Then he showed me his perfected posture. It amazed me. His body became a column of pure light and radiance. His mastery of yoga was not a physical attainment, but achieved through abandonment of ego, self-identification and pride.

Following the path of many yogis before me who faced equally humiliating and ego-defying exercises imposed upon them by their teachers, I gave up struggling against what I thought was a ridiculous waste of my time. I surrendered. Surrender to the teacher is the most important part of learning anything sacred. You have to let go of your ego and accept the authority of one who knows more than you. As an American, this was extremely hard for me.

When I finally allowed myself to accept the method of learning imposed on

Young Sanskrit Students in Haridwar, India

me, I placed all my attention on mindfully experiencing the pure sounds of Sanskrit. I observed that they had a sublimely pleasant effect on my nervous system. I discovered a deep bliss vibrating from the core of my being. And I came to love that simple practice of chanting the primordial sounds of Sanskrit without worrying about what they meant or how much progress I was making.

Eventually, I realized the method behind my teacher's madness. By continuous, daily chanting of Sanskrit, I experienced it's energizing force. I found by pronouncing the Sanskrit syllables with conscious attention on making the sounds correctly, I'd feel the "line of energy" they'd each open within my central nervous system—freeing me from emotional blockages. After chanting repetitively for hour-long sessions, my body felt so full that I didn't need to take many breaths. I'd sink instead into a deeply silent, breathless space. My entire body would be flooded with life force and my mind and emotions were calm, in a state of pure equanimity.

Time disappeared in that tiny cottage at the end of a narrow lane in Calcutta. Once I let go of needing to be an accomplished scholar, I became a beginner.

Then at the end of six months, my teacher finally said, "Now your voice has *shakti* in it. Now your voice has energy and power in it. Now I can teach you."

That moment became a revelation for me. I knew then that Sanskrit is not an old, dead, classical language that only accomplished academics can decipher. Instead, it became for me a living technology for awakening higher states of consciousness, understanding the subtle laws of creation, and attaining advanced states of meditation leading to enlightenment.

I spent five years in India receiving the traditional transmission of Sanskrit as sacred sound and meeting many saints and masters of yoga. In my meetings and studies, I discovered that Sanskrit (at the basis of the formal practices of yoga) transmutes the body and mind from the identification with the ego as the separate I-sense to the dawning of a presence that fills the being with transcendental light.

Twelve years after meeting Krishna Narayan in Nepal and hearing Sanskrit for the first time, I earned a masters degree in Sanskrit and a doctorate in Religious Studies and devised a method of teaching Sanskrit, which I coined *Sanskrit for Yogis.*

The *Sanskrit for Yogis* method relies on the simple and profound tradition of imparting the language of enlightenment orally from teacher-to-student instruction as I learned from my teachers in Nepal and India. Its purpose is to cultivate a refined opening of the subtle physiology, leading to the awakening of higher states of awareness, the goal of yoga and meditation.

Dr. Katy with Vedic Priest at Gangotri, source of the Ganges River.

Pilgrims on Chardham Yatra, Haridwar.

Chapter One

Sanskrit, the Language of Yoga & Enlightenment

"Oh best Mother, best river, best Goddess Sarasvati, can we exist without the power of expression? Oh Mother! Create for us language."

~ Rig Veda 2.41.16-18

Ancient invocations at Yamunotri, source of River Yamuna.

During the two years I studied Vedic Sanskrit with my teacher in Calcutta, I experienced the city's most recent past, as the capital of Britain's colonial rule of India. During their forced reign, the British made two great impositions upon India. The first was the compulsion to convert Hindus to Christianity, and the second was to administer law and subjugation for the profit of the empire.

In both cases, they encountered an obstacle in translating their authority to Hindus who were devoted to a different law encoded in their Sanskrit law books. If the British were to conquer the hearts and minds of India, they needed to translate Sanskrit and understand its application.

To this end, the Boden Professor of Sanskrit chair—the oldest in the Western world—was established at Oxford University in 1860. Lieutenant Colonel Joseph Boden (who'd served in the East India Company) donated the endowment, motivated by an intense personal desire to convert Hindus to Christianity. While that project largely failed, Sanskrit was converted from a living language to a "studied" academic language.

Today Indian children are taught Sanskrit in schools in the same way we learn any foreign language. They hate it. It's too difficult—especially compared with the traditional Vedic method of learning Sanskrit, which is natural and easy. The language has been colonized.

The British may have failed to convert anyone to Christianity, but they converted the Vedic system of education away from its subjective, integral style. Learning shifted from oral to written, from subjective to objective, and the heart of India's *sanatana dharma*, Sanskrit, fell its victim.

After the establishment of the Boden chair, Sanskrit became on par with "dead, classical" languages like Latin and Greek. Yet something good came out of Sanskrit being brought onto the world linguistic stage—a new field of study was born called "philology" (the comparative study of language)—wherein Sanskrit reigned as its queen.

Although Sanskrit had been stripped its status in Indian education, it became the "jewel in the crown" within the field of comparative linguistics, standing out as the giant among all the world's languages. Scholars discovered, confirmed and affirmed Sanskrit as the source of all Indo-European languages. And the best among philologists, F. Max Muller, declared, "Sanskrit is the Mother of all languages."

That means if you speak English, French, German, Russian or any European language (with the exception of Hungarian) as well as many of the modern Indian languages and Persian, Sanskrit is at the root. At some point in history there may have been a common language, Sanskrit, spoken by a vast population of people spread out over a diverse geography. As a result, many, many of our words in English derive from Sanskrit roots. If when you come across Sanskrit words in yoga, you can make that connection, the meaning of the seemingly foreign words becomes familiar.

"Sanskrit" is the anglicized form of the word for the sacred language of yoga, *Samskrta*, consisting of two parts, *sam* and *krta*. *Sam* sounds like our English word "sum," and has the same meaning of "total."

Krta has the same meaning as our English word, "created."

Together, the word *Samskrta* means "created" or "made" out of the state of the "total," or "unity."

Samskrta is not just a word that has a symbolic meaning. It's an expression of the structure of the material world that's echoed in modern science. Quantum physics, for example, reveals in String theory that everything in the objective, material universe is vibrating at its core. What seems solid and unchanging in our physical world is actually moving so quickly that it appears to be standing still. This implies that if you were subtle enough in your awareness, you'd be able to "hear" and "see" those vibrations and replicate them with your voice.

The theory that distinguishable and varied vibrations form the core of all created matter lies at the basis of the Sanskrit language. Most importantly, it's a technology that achieves something remarkable. By replicating the subtle sounds of creation with the human voice, one becomes unified with all aspects of the physical and subtle universe.

The ancient sages of India (known as *rishis* or "seers of ultimate truth") made this discovery of Sanskrit by their attainment of extraordinary states of intelligent perception through meditation, permitting them to see and hear the subtle "strings of code" at the basis of creation. They recorded these arrangements of sounds in their speech, committed them to memory, and passed them down to their disciples to preserve them for posterity. The sounds they heard were combinations of the 50 Sanskrit syllables, forming the corpus of the Veda.

Veda comes from the same Sanskrit verbal root from which we get our English word, "video." Just like a video is a projection of pixilations of light and sound, this world is nothing other than a diversified array of vibrations, distinguishing themselves only by different combinations of sounds and rhythms.

The *rishis* saw in their mind's eye that these subtle sounds abide at the very source of all things manifest in nature—like trees, rocks, plants, animals and human beings. They then recorded what they saw and heard in the form of rhythmic speech, or *mantras*, which make up what are sometimes called the "hymns" of the Veda. You could say that the chants of the Veda are recordings of the way the created world arises, mutates, and dissolves.

These *mantras*, or pure forms of sound, are likened to sonic building blocks that form the underlying architecture of both the visible and invisible or subtle universe. When you replicate these *mantras* exactly as they have been passed down orally in the Vedic tradition, they cultivate your subtle nervous system to that of the extraordinarily intelligent and perceptive *rishis*.

The oral transmission of nature's vibrational code has been kept alive for thousands of generations in India through the sacred guru-disciple relationship. The teacher enlivens the liberating energy in the student's body-

Ancient bells.

mind through the constant repetition of Sanskrit. Beginning when a child is just four or five-years-old, she memorizes hundreds of thousands of rhythmic patterns by mimicking her teacher's tone, pattern of breath, and pronunciation. This continues daily for twelve years, during which time the child's nervous system is cultured to perceive more subtle levels of reality—from the physical to the vital inner core of all things. Purified by the continuous pulse of healing sound, her body itself effortlessly channels a higher light. And through the breath's regulation by proper pronunciation of the Sanskrit syllables, her mind is directed to a more clairvoyant and clairaudient perception of conscious thought.

When the child-disciple reaches physical maturity by the age of 16 or so, her very body has become a beacon of healing, vitalizing, and bliss-bestowing light by this ancient method of Sanskrit chanting. Such an enlightened individual is invaluable to everything within her vicinity. She instills an environment of peace by her very presence, fostering the growth of positive human values in the society at large. The plants and animals likewise respond in harmony with such a state of being.

For this reason, the *Hatha Yoga Pradipika* asserts that "the union of the mind with pure sound is the highest and most subtle form of yoga." Chanting Sanskrit is an essential and complementary practice to yoga *asana*, *pranayama*, and meditation, the benefit of which is for a much larger field of influence beyond the physical body and mind.

I didn't fully understand the goal of my yoga, meditation and chanting practices until I spent several months living with a friend's grandmother, Nani, in a small central Indian village along the Narmada River while conducting my doctoral dissertation research.

Village homes are crowded scenes. I had no personal space and even slept in a bed with five other women. I understood why historically yogis had to run away to the Himalayas to meditate. You simply can't find a place to practice without being disturbed in village India!

I discovered an abandoned storeroom, however, in Nani's house that became my practice space. I thought I'd escape notice there and conduct my daily practices without interruption. But I could only enjoy one day unnoticed before my secret was out.

The following morning, as I swooped my arms above my head in the first *vinyasa* of my sun salutation, I noticed a small crowd had gathered outside the room. Many sets of eyes were peeping through the window. Ignoring them, I continued with my yoga, chanting, and meditation practice. I thought they'd get the "hint" and leave me to my self for a while.

Yet once my practice was over and I left the room for breakfast, the crowd persisted, stopping me with a multitude of varied requests.

"My son is getting married. Will you look at the photos of potential brides for him?"

"My mother-in-law is very sick. Could you pronounce a healing *mantra* for her?"

"*Didi* (sister), will you bless our seeds? We want to have a good crop this year. Last year was terrible."

I found this a truly strange spectacle. I had no idea why these villagers felt that I could help with their problems, when Nani made it clear. "You are a *yogini* who's come to the village. Your presence here is a blessing for the people and the land. Such a *yogini* purifies the place by her meditation and her chanting of Vedas. She brings God here."

My attitude changed from then on. The practice of yoga, meditation, and chanting Sanskrit *mantras* took on an entirely different meaning for me. It inspires, uplifts and enlivens nature and its inhabitants, establishing a positive and healthy environment for everyone within the vicinity of the practicing yogi. I've come to appreciate these practices not only for my own peace of mind, but also for peace on Earth.

Scholar in residence, Ramakrishna Institute of Culture, Calcutta, 1992

Chapter Two

Name and Form in Sanskrit and in the Practice of Yoga Asana

The divine name is the pure nectar of bliss.

~ Swami Muktananda

Many times students will ask me what a word in Sanskrit means in English. I myself spent many years pouring over a thick dictionary in vain attempts at rendering the intricate, poetic beauty of Sanskrit into plain, direct and comprehensible English. Yet how can you describe what chocolate tastes like if you've never tasted chocolate?

Throughout my traditional studies with teachers in India, I had ample opportunities to distinguish the noticeable and unique feelings of each of the 50 syllables in Sanskrit and their combinations. I'd feel specific channels of energy in my subtle body open when I'd pronounce a letter or a mantra perfectly. I wondered if the current of energy and its directional pattern contained within every word in Sanskrit had some relationship to the shape of what it represented in nature.

Through self-study, I observed when I'd say the Sanskrit name for a yoga posture, for example, I'd detect a flow of energy along a circuit of channels in my body. When I'd make the shape of the posture physically, its alignment matched the subtle energetic current.

In Sanskrit, the name and form of anything are identical. This is not the case with modern languages. The words we express in English don't participate in the vibrational structure of those things. Instead, they are symbolic.

For example, if I were to gather a group of English speakers and ask them to tell me the first word that arises in their mind when I say "apple," they'd offer so many different responses. Some will think, "red." Others will think, "crunchy." Still others will think, "tree, juicy, computer, and so on."

Everyone would conjure a different association of just one word in English. I'd be obliged to explain what I mean by "apple." I'd have to use many more words to create a symbolic vision in everyone's mind until we could all arrive at a common understanding. Even then, there'd be the possibility for different symbolic associations. Imagine in one conversation how much misunderstanding there is! It's no wonder we don't have peace on Earth. There is so much division in our language.

In Sanskrit, this is not the case. Instead, the name of something is always identical with the form.

There are probably a hundred different words for "apple" in Sanskrit. If I were to say "apple" in Sanskrit, the word I'd invoke would match the vibrational structure of the kind of apple I had in mind. In other words, the syllables would replicate the sounds that constitute the subtle, energetic structure of the object being spoken. Everyone would understand immediately what I was talking about. Their minds would unify around the vibrations of the word/object.

Boy selling plums, Haridwar.

Because name and form are identical in Sanskrit, pronouncing the Sanskrit names for the yoga postures becomes vitally important to your progress in the practice of yoga. This is because the name embodies the energetic shape that's replicated in the gross physical body, which is at its source a vibrating mass of sound pulsations.

Specifically, these sound pulsations are localized along 107 points on our physical body called *marmas*. If you've ever had an acupuncture treatment, you'll understand what a *marma* is. An acupuncturist determines where the energetic block is located in the internal structure of the body that is causing the symptom. She then inserts a needle into one or more points on the body's surface that connects with the area of stagnancy through subtle channels. The pressure on those points sends an energetic flow from the surface to the inner and subtle structures of the body, enlivening a connection that promotes health and wholeness.

In Chinese medicine, these energetic gateways that open to the deep recesses of the body are called "meridian points," which derive from the *marma* points put forth by the older Indian medical system of Ayurveda. Ayurveda maps a set of 107 sensitive *marma* points on the body's surface that connect via subtle channels (*nadis*) to the deeper energetic centers of the nervous system known as *cakras*. Each *marma* point has a Sanskrit syllable associated with it. When a Sanskrit syllable is pronounced perfectly it sends an energetic current through its *marma* point, enlivening a pathway to invigorate the core of the central nervous system.

When you say the name for a yoga posture in Sanskrit, you emit a pulse of *prana* or life force along a series of *marma* points associated with those sounds. The physical alignment of a posture, therefore, has a "sonic shape" that correlates with it and replicates the energetic core of the thing in nature your body is forming.

The ancient yogis observed nature very closely. They noted the pattern of breath in creatures and plants when their bodies formed certain shapes. The yogis replicated those patterns with their own bodies, matching their breath to the breath of the animal they imitated. The Sanskrit name for that posture perfectly matches the "shape" of the being's life force as it corresponds to the relevant *marma* points on the human body. Pronouncing the Sanskrit name for the posture and feeling its energetic flow,

Therefore, is the power behind your yoga practice to achieve its ultimate goal: *absolute unity with everything in nature.*

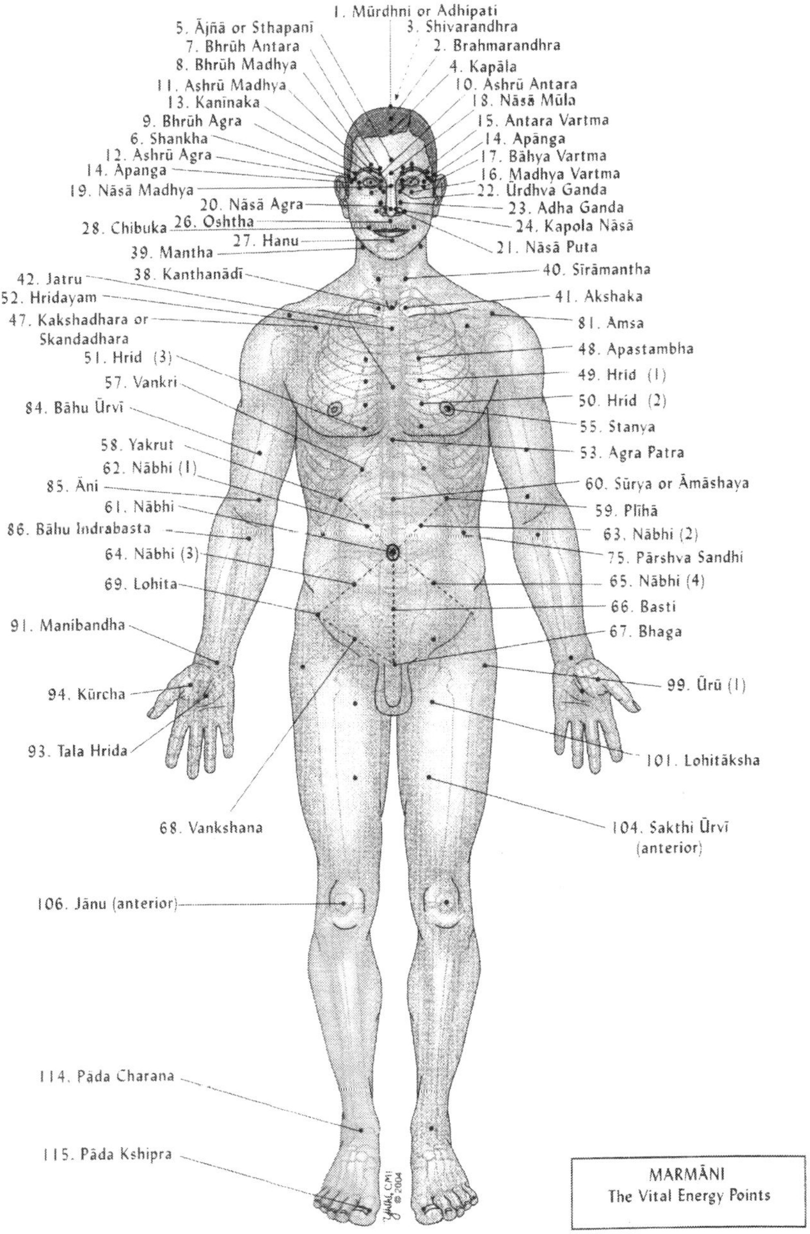

Image of Marma Points on the Body courtesy of Vasant D. Lad and Anisha Durve, Marma Points of Ayurveda.

For example, the name for "cobra pose" in Sanskrit is *bhujanga* consisting of the syllables *bham, um, jam, gam, nam* and *am*. *Bhujanga* is the physical and sonic form of a specific type of cobra with its body coiled and its hood extended. The syllables that make up the name for such a creature are identical to its form. The *asana* shape replicates the physical form of such a snake, whereas the Sanskrit syllables making up its name replicate its sonic form traced along the *marma* points associated with those syllables.

The *marma* points that correspond with *bham* are located in the central, lower abdomen. *Um* are the points right behind the ears. The first syllable of the cobra pose, *bhum*, therefore, traces an energetic flow of *prana* from the center of the chest to the point right behind the ears.

The *marma* points in the center of the palms of the hands and feet connect with the *nam* sound. *Gam* and *jam* vibrate in the center of the right and left forearms respectively and *am* is at the top of the head, in the center of the skull.

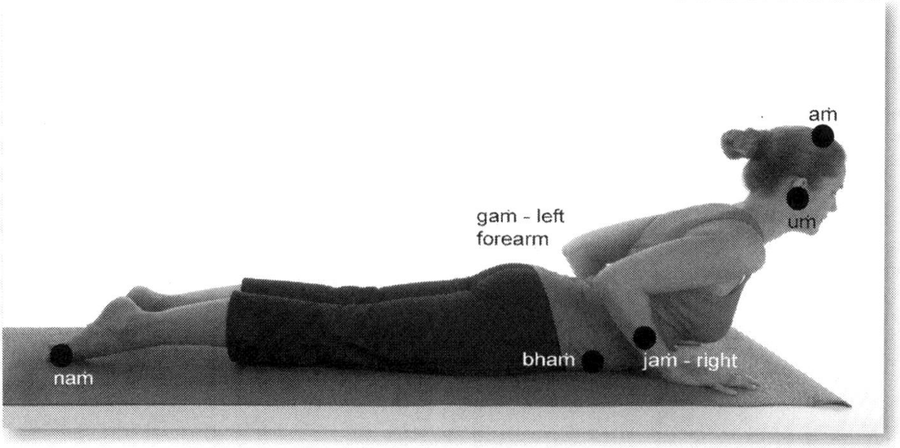

Cobra Posture with Marmas (photo courtesy of Mindy Arbuckle, 2018).

Envision yourself making the form of a cobra. First you feel the energy flow from the *marma* points in the center of the chest to the back of the ears. Then you lightly press your palms into the earth, extending your feet outward behind the body. You'll then feel the energy rise up through the center of the hands and feet to the forearms to the top of the head.

Every Sanskrit name for the yoga postures creates a similar kind of sonic shape traced along the *marma* points, which match the energetic flow of all forms in nature that you can replicate with your body and breath. And interestingly, the cues that yoga teachers provide to properly align you in the posture follow the sequence of syllables exactly. When learning the yoga postures and how to teach them properly, it is indispensable, therefore, to master the Sanskrit names and their associated *marma* points.

I discovered the connection between the *marma* points, the Sanskrit syllables, and the names for the yoga postures quite by accident. I had often been asked by well-meaning yoga teachers to help them with their Sanskrit pronunciation of the yoga *asanas*. Simply saying the names without the full experience of the energy contained within them seemed unfulfilling to me. There had to be a deeper significance. Pronouncing the names correctly had to serve the goal of yoga: *to establish the body, breath, and mind in unity.*

I wondered if the ancient treatises on yoga could shed light on the relationship between the Sanskrit names of the yoga postures and the pattern of energy generated by pronouncing them. I first turned to Patanjali's *Yoga Sutras* as they are the most important source of traditional knowledge about Yoga. Yet he only devotes three *sutras* to the explanation of *asana*.

He states:

> *Asana should be steady (sthira) and comfortable (sukha). It is achieved by reducing the restless tendency and by identifying with infinity (ananta). Then one remains undisturbed by dualities.*
>
> ~ Yoga Sutras 2:46-248 ~

Apart from these three *sutras*, Patanjali doesn't describe the myriad postures that contemporary yogis practice. He provides no instruction toward the attainment of proper *asana*. Instead, Patanjali devotes his treatise to the subject of *samadhi* as the goal of yoga, realized through the repetition of the supreme *mantra, Oṁ*. Sacred sound in Sanskrit clearly takes precedence over physical practices in classical yoga.

The *Hatha Yoga Pradipika* of Svatmarama deals more specifically with the bodily basis of yoga. Hatha Yoga, stemming from the Tantric traditions made popular and public in medieval India, espouses the sacred power contained within the human body and nervous system. The body is a gateway leading to the attainment of enlightened immortality, obtained through mastery of hearing the inner, mystical sounds resonant within the central nervous system. Svatmarama concludes, in fact: "*the union of the mind with pure sound is the highest form of yoga.*" All the cleansing rituals, yoga postures, breathing practices and meditation disciplines described in the *Hatha Yoga Pradipika* simply allow the yogi to listen more deeply to the vibrations abiding at the source of Being and ultimately merge his awareness with them.

My quest for understanding the relationship between the Sanskrit names for the yoga postures was still not complete. My inquiry led me to the works of the 10th century Kashmir Shaivite mystic, Abhinavagupta, whose massive

Tantraloka contained profound linkages and explanations of the Sanskrit syllables and the structures of the subtle human physiology. I discovered that Abhinavagupta's descriptions of *kundalini*, the *cakra* system, the *nadis*, and *marmas* and their relationship to the energetics of Sanskrit was based in part on *Dhanurveda*, the ancient system of Vedic martial arts.

The *Sushruta Samhita* (c. 4th century), the principle text of Dhanurveda, maps 107 vital points on the human body that distribute the flow of life force or *prana* from the surface to the inner recesses of the physiology. The task of a fighter was to attack or defend these gateways that hold the body's energy intact. To prepare for battle, the preparatory exercises were designed to strengthen the connection between the vital points and the energetic core of the body. These exercises remain alive today in the South Indian *kalari* tradition of martial arts and in the *vinyasa* style of yoga.

Sushruta's work formed the basis of the medical system of Ayurveda, which developed alongside the Vedic martial arts tradition. Originally, Ayurveda was vibrational medicine and *vaidyas* (Ayurvedic physicians) routinely prescribed the chanting of Sanskrit *mantras* to prevent illness or treat specific ailments, regarded as energetic imbalances. In Ayurveda, the 107 vital points (*marmas*) of Dhanurveda were associated with specific Sanskrit syllables that enlivened their energetic current and promoted health. By intoning the pure sounds of Sanskrit and regulating the breath, the *marmas* absorbed the healing vibrations, directing them to the inner core of the body via the channels of the subtle nervous system to restore balance.

Finally, through the lore of his students, I learned that the great grandmaster of modern yoga, Sri Krishnamacarya, instructed his disciples to chant the entire Sanskrit alphabet while holding themselves in yoga *asana*. In light of all my findings, especially in Dhanurveda and its survival in the South Indian martial arts and yoga practices (the region that Krishnamacarya hailed from), I discovered a profound reason to pronounce the Sanskrit names for the yoga postures: *to awaken and enliven the inner core of the body, leading to effortless meditation and samadhi.*

Pronouncing the Sanskrit name for the posture and feeling its energetic flow, therefore, is the power behind your yoga practice to achieve its ultimate goal. Despite my initial skepticism, I now appreciate the absolute necessity of pronouncing the Sanskrit names of the *asanas* themselves as a portal to the spiritual freedom that yoga promises.

Chapter Three

The Identity of Meaning and Feeling in Sanskrit

"Feel the Presence in the heart: not in the front, not in the back, not in the side, not above, and not below, but in the core of the very existence."

~ Sri Sri Ravi Shankar

In a modern language like English, you have to add feeling or emphasis to the words you speak in order to express the meaning you desire. For example, I can say, "I love you," with passion, with sarcasm, with tenderness, or with anger. The words themselves don't exhibit feeling. You have to add that yourself to articulate what you wish to communicate emotionally. You can also conceal what you really feel by manipulating the tone and emotion of your words.

In Sanskrit, however, meaning and feeling are identical. You can't pronounce a Sanskrit word perfectly without transmitting a specific feeling that arises from its syllables. Its vibrations, like music, present a feeling to the nervous system that cannot be altered or denied. That feeling naturally triggers a meaning.

Chanting and listening to the pure vibrations of Sanskrit awaken a profound inner feeling triggered by speaking and hearing. Higher states of consciousness increase through continuous and refined aural sensory contact. The Vedic teachings hold that by developing our most sensitive and subtle sense of hearing, our knowledge capacity expands.

In Vedic education, nothing can be taught. You don't learn a subject by referring to sources outside yourself. Instead, knowledge results by awakening your own inherent capacity to know everything within your highly sophisticated nervous system.

Neuroscience claims that we only utilize ten percent of our brain's capacity for knowledge. According to Vedic thought, the cultured feeling of vibration through listening—*nada yoga*—awakens the remaining ninety percent that's lying dormant within your nervous system. For example, if I want to understand algebra, I simply need to enliven my capacity to know algebra that already exists within my intelligent nervous system. The Vedas claim that awakening results from the repetitive call and response chanting at the heart of Vedic education.

For this reason, the sacred teachings of yoga are not "read" like books in English, but are "felt," arousing your own intrinsic faculty to know through the vibrations of Sanskrit. To culture "feeling intelligence," all the important scriptures were always composed in Sanskrit and orally transmitted from teacher to student. Each word in Sanskrit opens a new pathway of feeling, allowing a student to relate with whole body, mind and breath to the subject. All intelligence, therefore, is emotional intelligence.

What Western academics describe as Sanskrit "texts," like Patanjali's *Yoga Sutras*, therefore, are not the same as published books. We read books objectively, not experiencing the words with all of our senses beyond the sense of sight. When we read words on a page, our mind creates a division from the words themselves and what we interpret them to mean. In contrast, when you listen and repeat the Sanskrit words of a "text," your feeling capacity allows you to totally identify with the subject, expanding your range of perception and knowledge about it. For this reason, all the liberating knowledge throughout the history of India was always memorized orally.

It's said when Alexander the Great conquered northeastern India, he approached the most learned man he could find. "Bring me all your books," Alexander commanded, "for I wish to house them in my great library." The scholar obliged by presenting him with a basket full of decaying palm leaves. Alexander was very disappointed. "After all I have heard about India's great intellectual achievements, this stinking heap is all you have to show for them!"

The learned man listened patiently to Alexander's rants and then responded, "We need not contain our sacred knowledge in books. Everything is inscribed perfectly in our hearts by memory."

Always passed down orally from teacher to student, the *Yoga Sutras* in Sanskrit embody a state of consciousness with a distinct feeling that's communicated to your nervous system via the sound of the *sutras*. By listening to and repeating the ordered syllables that make up the first chapter of the *Yoga Sutras*, for example, you attain the state of yogic union or *samadhi*. You don't objectively contemplate the philosophical principles expressed in the text. Instead, the precise arrangement of the syllables unfolds the actual goal of yoga in your nervous system.

In contrast, when you read or listen to the *sutras* in English translation, the intended feeling is entirely lost. For example, the first *sutra* is often translated, "Now begins the discipline that is Yoga." The only meaning that line conveys to us is that a subject is being introduced to preface a more meaningful discussion to come later. There is no feeling that arises in you from these words except perhaps boredom.

Yet in Sanskrit, the first word of any scripture embodies the precise meaning and feeling of what it expounds. In the *Yoga Sutras*, the goal of the first chapter is to establish the yogi in the heightened state of *samadhi*. The meaning and feeling of the first word, *atha*, communicates the experience of *samadhi* directly to the nervous system.

Take a moment to experience this principle.

The first syllable of *atha* is pronounced "uh." Say that sound a few times, contrasting it with "aah." When you say "uh," you feel a contraction inside. In contrast, "aah" creates a feeling of release and expansion. You don't say, "Uh, I'm in love." You say instead, "Aah, I'm in love," and, "Uh, I stubbed my toe!"

"Uh" is a contraction. Because it's a contracting feeling, it communicates the meaning "no," "not" or "negation." It's like in English when we say something is "atypical." It means it's "not typical."

"Uh" is the first vowel of the 16 vowels of Sanskrit, each one corresponding with the 16 phases of the waxing/waning moon. Each phase of the moon has a particular emotional quality associated with it that's communicated via a vowel sound in Sanskrit.

The first syllable of *atha* correlates with the new moon. During the new moon phase we experience an absence of light. With that absence, we can see the totality. We see the fullness of the sky and stars in the cosmos.

Likewise, when we contract deep inside ourselves with the sound, "uh," we're pulled beyond the limitations of this gross physical form. We experience a state of pure being and inner freedom. Even though it connotes something negative, "not, negation or no", it really has to do with "not this." You are not your body, your feelings, or your thoughts. Rather you're part of something much deeper and much more expansive on an inner level. That's "uh."

The next syllable of *atha* is "tha." It's not like "tha" in "thank you." In Sanskrit, you pronounce this sound by bringing the tongue in between the teeth. Then you drop the jaw straight down like a ventriloquist doll, "thuh." It's where we get the English word, "thud."

As you repeat this sound, the energy feels like it's being pulled down. When you drop something, the force of gravity causes it to fall. "Thuh" both feels and means "gravity", which is the cause for your bondage to the earth.

Together, if you say "uh-thuh" it feels and means "no gravity," "not bound" or "no bondage." It means and feels like freedom. If you aren't subject to the laws of gravity, you're liberated. When are you free? Are you free when you mind is stuck in the past? Or when you're projecting onto the future? You're free right now in this moment. That's why the translation of *atha* is "now."

The goal of yoga is summarized and experienced in that first word. If you can feel the pulse of the present moment contained in the Sanskrit word *atha*, you're established in the state of union that is yoga. You're totally and perfectly free. The remaining *sutras* unfold the experience of the present moment so you can easily recognize it instinctively when your mind takes you out of the state. The *Yoga Sutras*, therefore, contains the vibrational code that allows you to attain its goal effortlessly within your own body and mind through the vehicle of Sanskrit as sacred sound.

Chapter Four

Pronunciation of Sanskrit and the Preservation of Prana

"When we think of a particular letter of the Sanskrit alphabet or a combination of these letters, each produces certain thoughts, certain mental vibrations…Each syllable has within it a particular ray of consciousness."

~ Swami Veda Bharati

One thing I noticed about my Sanskrit teacher (and most brahmins I've encountered) was his inexhaustible energy. It was once Navaratri, and my teacher participated in celebrating these "Nine Nights of the Goddess" by conducting a series of Vedic fire ceremonies together with a team of Vedic priests. All was going fine until one of the priests made a mistake. It was a tiny mistake, but nevertheless a mistake and the entire ceremony needed to be redone. The priests who'd been chanting for hours now would have to stay up all night and repeat the entire procedure.

I would have been exhausted at the prospect, but instead after more than 8 hours of continuous chanting in Sanskrit they glowed with a kind of effervescent energy. None of them seemed tired in the least. In fact, it appeared to me as the hours passed their voices became even more vigorous. And no one felt like sleeping when the dawn approached.

There's a noticeable difference between spending an hour speaking in English and an hour chanting in Sanskrit. In the former case, you find your energy depleted. That's because we have no mechanism in our modern languages to recapture the life force that gets expelled with our exhalation as we speak. In the latter case of Sanskrit, however, the simple rules of pronunciation are designed to redirect the *prana* back into the physical and subtle body.

As you exhale through your mouth, you'll notice that the breath passes over five distinct regions: the larynx, the soft palate, the hard palate, the teeth, and the lips. Each sound made in Sanskrit stimulates one of these regions, which are each a *marma* point that opens a *pranic* pathway, or *nadi*, that sends energy that would otherwise be exhaled back into the subtle body. Your speech in Sanskrit, therefore, serves as a powerful form of *pranayama* that preserves and enlivens your life force.

Unlike most modern languages, the arrangement of the Sanskrit alphabet follows the evolutionary scheme of nature. While its vowels correspond with the "states" of higher consciousness and what some religions have described as the "angelic" realms, the consonants replicate the myriad of Earth's life forms, from the amphibian, insect, bird, rodent, to the mammal kingdoms. Since humans are the only creatures who can recreate all the sounds of nature through our unique organs of speech, the voice serves as a bridge, connecting heaven and earth. While our language often promotes misunderstanding and conflict, Sanskrit, when pronounced precisely, best achieves the ultimate goal of all yoga practice—the total union of opposites.

Vowels form the core of Sanskrit's alphabet. These sounds are made without the assistance of the organs of speech (the tongue, the teeth, or the lips). Babies in their most innocent state of consciousness intone vowel sounds — "aaah," "eeeh," "oooh." At some point in our early childhood (around the "terrible two's"), we realize our separation from our mother and say our first consonants—"maah" and "daah." (Or more often, "me!") The duality of consonants ("to sound together") expresses the psychology of our separation. As distinct individuals, we often find ourselves in life attempting to be understood, to connect with others and our world. This is why if we have a good conversation with someone, we say, "I connected with so-and-so." Or, if not, "We had a disconnect."

But the Sanskrit language recognizes that just as consonants are the sounds of separation, they also serve to re-connect us to the innocent state of unity we experienced as infants. For this reason, Sanskrit is called the "mother of all languages," because it returns us to the source of life, which according to the Yogic point of view is silent, pure Being.

This is how it works:

The Sanskrit vowels and consonants are found to be especially soothing to the mind and nervous system. They are most often "natural" sounds we make as we inhale and exhale, such as *so* (inhale) and *ham* (exhale). As the breath travels out of the body, we make language when the organs of our speech—the larynx, the base of the tongue, the tip of the tongue, the teeth, and lips—touch these five regions that connect mind with body. When precisely pronounced, the consonant sounds of Sanskrit penetrate these nerve centers in the head cavity like an acupuncture needle, directing *prana* to their corresponding body parts and nerve centers.

1. The *Guttural* region is in the throat.
2. The *Palatal* region is across the roof of the mouth
3. The *Retroflex* region is located on the "ridge" or "soft palate" just before the teeth
4. The *Dental* region is when the tip of the tongue makes contact with directly with the upper teeth
5. The *Labial* region is through the lips

Just as there are five regions and organs of speech, there are five energetic centers in the body, from the base of the spine to the heart. Each one of these centers resonates with the energies of the five elements (earth, water, fire, air, and ether), the five animal kingdoms (amphibian, insect, birds, rodents, and mammals), and the five classifications of Sanskrit consonants. By recreating the sounds of our world, we align ourselves with the rhythms and melodies of nature. We also do this when we practice yoga *asanas*, which also often mimic the animals of the natural world (cobra, frog, fish, eagle, elephant, and so on).

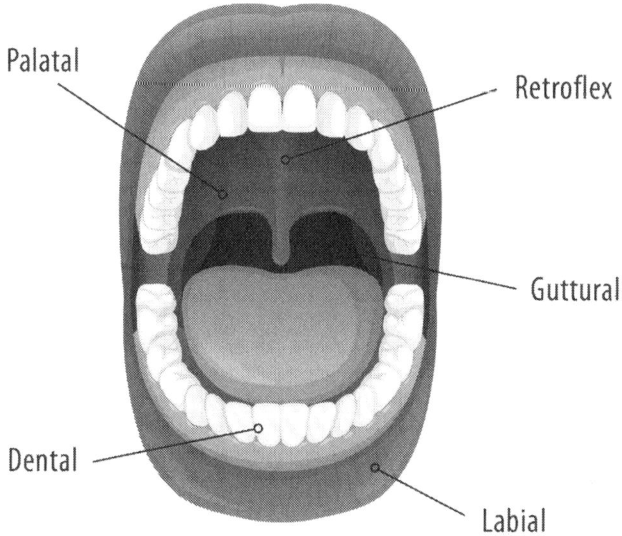

Five Regions of Speech in Sanskrit.

Every Sanskrit syllable, therefore, opens the *marma* points in your vocal cavity and along the surface of your body, to direct *prana* through the channels or *nadis* that connect the *marmas* to the deep internal energetic centers or *cakras.* They also establish a resonance between the vibrations of your subtle body and the forms in nature that correspond with the Sanskrit syllables at their core.

As I mentioned earlier, the 16 vowel sounds connect your emotional states with the phases of the moon. The 25 consonants connect your five sense organs with the five regions of speech, the five ways of sensing, the five sense objects, and the five elements in nature. The four semi-vowels orient you to the four directions in nature and link the flow of your spinal fluid with the upward flow of sap in trees and plants. The three sibilant sounds enliven the three nerve channels along the central axis of the body: the i*da, pingala* and *susumna nadis* that intersect at the location of the seven *cakras.* The two final sounds allow your body, mind and breath to dissolve back into the primal state of unified consciousness at death.

*Energetic centers (*cakras*) and their corresponding Sanskrit syllables.*

Sanskrit Alphabet

अ a	आ ā	इ i	ई ï	उ u	ऊ ū
ऋ r	ॠ r̄	ऌ !	ए e	ऐ ai	ओ o
औ au	क ka	ख kha	ग ga	घ gha	ङ na
च ca	छ cha	ज ja	झ jha	ञ ña	ट ta
ठ tha	ड da	ढ dha	ण na	त ta	थ tha
द da	ध dha	न na	प pa	फ pha	ब ba
भ bha	म ma	य ya	र ra	ल la	व va
	श śa	ष ṣa	स sa	ह ha	

Here is a simple chart of the arrangement of the Sanskrit syllables.

Author meditating at Dunagiri, India.

Chapter Five

Devanagari: The Sacred Calligraphy of Sanskrit

> *"Writing is divine, inherently holy, with powers to teach the highest mysteries; writing is the speech of the gods, the ideal form of beauty."*
>
> ~ *John Stevens, Sacred Calligraphy of the East*

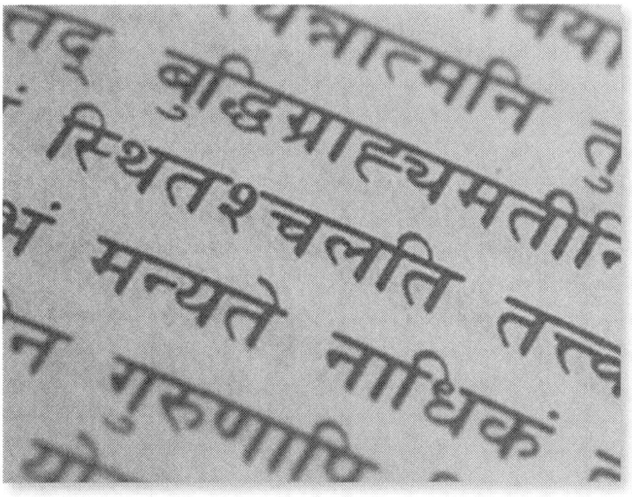

During one of the years I lived in India, I found myself traveling by open jeep through the interiors of Madhya Pradesh (which at the time was India's largest and least developed state). On pilgrimage to the source of the holy Narmada River at Amarkanthak, I had to traverse through many thick jungles, unpaved roads, and up steep inclines to get there—and through regions, my driver warned me, populated with man-eating tigers!

I didn't have the chance to encounter one of these magnificent beasts, but I met instead some really colorful characters along the way. In particular, one group of people who call themselves *Ram Namis* ("Those Rapt in the Name of God") made a deep impression on me.

Perhaps in no time during the history of India has anyone taken the physically redemptive power of Ram's name—the entire essence of his sacred narrative in seed syllable form—as literally as the Ramnamis of central India. By inscribing the name of Ram in the *devanagari* script on the body, it elevated an entire community of untouchables out of untouchability.

These people express their devotion to their chosen expression of God, Lord Ram, by tattooing his name in the Sanskrit script, *devanagari,* all over their bodies. They print it on the fabric of the clothes they wear. The walls in their homes are covered with God's name. And they keep their mind solely focused on the Divine by continuously repeating, "Ram, Ram."

In these ways, they saturate themselves with the presence of God—from skin to soul. The miracle of Ram's omnipresence is embodied everywhere.

This practice is in imitation of Lord Ram's best devotee, Hanuman, who when questioned if he really had any faith in God, tore open his chest to reveal the name of Ram permanently etched on his heart.

Likewise these villagers believe that by tattooing their entire bodies with the letters of Ram's name, they become one with him. This is, in part, due to the geometric energy of the Sanskrit letters written in the *devanagari* script—which is sacrosanct. It is the container of divinity—the embodied universe in sacred geometry.

Likhta Japa master, Garwahl, India.

Devanagari—"divine" (*deva*) and "city" (*nagari*)—refers to one of the systems used to write down the oral Sanskrit syllables. It translates as "city of the gods," or more loosely, "the container of divine light." Because of its precision, beauty, and depth, the Vedic sages believed Sanskrit did not evolve out of ordinary human experience, but through the very speech of the gods or "beings of light" (*deva/devi*). Sanskrit is the language with which the laws of nature and highly enlightened yogis communicate with each other and which describes the divine design of the cosmos itself.

The Sanskrit characters written in *devanagari* are, therefore, the outer symbols that express the intercommunication between human and divine. In the ancient days, *devanagari* adorned temple walls to attract the gods to earth as well as to inspire humans toward their unified nature. This is why *devanagari* is also called "divine temple writing." It's a kind of sacred graffiti.

Writing the Sanskrit letters in *devanagari* is a special form of meditation called *likhta japa* ("repetitive writing meditation"). The order of the strokes especially trains the mind to recognize specific flows of *prana* through the body. It trains you to recognize through eye/hand coordination the movement of energy currents pulsing through everything in creation.

The shapes of the script have a kind of musical quality to them, like Western musical notation, that conveys the movement of primordial sound. Although much of this knowledge is lost to us in the modern age, the shapes of the letters serve as pictographs for all the spiritual and terrestrial objects of the universe.

For example, *Oṁ* as it is written in *devanagari* conveys the shape of Shiva Nataraja, the god (law of nature) that dances this world into being, activating the three movements of life (creation, maintenance and destruction) embodied in the three syllables of AUM. For this reason, he's also called Omkareshwara, "The Lord Who Creates the World as *Oṁ*."

Compare the *devanagari* symbol of *Oṁ* with the shape of Shiva Nataraja. Name and form are identical (*figure 1*).

Shiva's limbs that extend to the left are the three "limbs" of the first part of *Oṁ*:

उ

(Figure 1) Shiva as Omkareshwara, the Om-maker.

His open hand to the right holds the drum of creation and is indicated by the tail pointing to the right in the *Oṁ* symbol:

ॐ

The crescent Moon that rests as a still point in Shiva's wild mane of hair is shown by the *candra bindu* ("moon drop") placed on the top of *Oṁ*, which is the "nasalization" sound in Sanskrit.

ँ

The circle of flames surrounding Shiva is the light of creation and the fire of destruction as in the first syllable of *Oṁ*—A:

अ

Your own body is a vibrating mass of sonic shapes, in the form of perfect geometry or *yantra. Yantras* consist of specific arrangements of shapes—circles, squares, and triangles—that expand your consciousness visually in the same way *mantras* do aurally. *Yantra* is visual *mantra,* embodying the inner, vibratory nature of creation.

The *devanagari* characters are *yantras.* The human body is a *yantra,* an intricate matrix of nerves and paths of energy. Your breath follows a pattern that forms a perfect shape. It's said that the whole world is a *yantra* in which all the shapes of the mountains, flowers, rivers, and clouds tell us the story of creation. The *devanagari* letters, just like the Sanskrit oral syllables, provide a meditative glimpse into the sublime beauty of nature's arrangement.

Following is a sample of the simple Sanskrit vowels in Sanskrit vowels in *devanagari* with the order of their strokes indicated (*figure 2*).

(Figure 2) Sanskrit vowels in devanagari.

Practice Writing Devanagari

Chapter Six

The Bliss of Chanting Sanskrit as Mantra

"As one continues to chant, the mind becomes saturated with the mantras and easily achieves one-pointedness. The heart is stabilized on its goal and begins to taste the joy which is the inner essence of the mantras…One realizes that the heart is the abode of deep peace, where love gushes."

~ Swami Muktananda

Sanskrit for Yogis immersion, Pavones Yoga Center (Costa Rica, 2016).

I'll never forget the first time I encountered the power of sacred sound. I was attending a *kirtan* (devotional singing) gathering led by my first yoga teacher, Divya Prabha, in Santa Barbara. As she began chanting *Oṁ namah shivaya*, I felt pulled in by the magnetism of the syllables and her voice. All my attention gravitated to the breath I took in, the melodious sounds I'd make on the exhale, and the slight gap between breaths before the chanting began again on the inhale.

As the chant continued, I felt myself losing ordinary consciousness. Instead a bigness in the form of a column of light grew inside from the base of my spine to beyond the top of my head. All I could feel was joy.

When it was over, I couldn't move from my seat. I'd grown up attending church as a child and had sung devotional songs that moved my heart. But this was something entirely different. I had no idea what the verse I'd just sung over and over again meant. The sounds themselves had a power prior to meaning.

Every one of the 50 syllables in the Sanskrit alphabet is a *mantra*. Consisting of two parts, "*man*" and "*tra*," *mantra* means, "that which extends (*tra*) the mind or heart (*man*)." *Mantra* establishes tranquility in mind and body by regulating the rhythm of the breath and silences the fluctuation of thoughts until only the Sanskrit syllable exits. In this way, *mantra* is, as yoga scholar Georg Feuerstein describes, "a vehicle of transcendence."

Just as *mantra* establishes resonance with the created world, it also serves as a vehicle for the mind to come to rest. For the mind, according to the *Hatha Yoga Pradipika*, is "like a serpent, forgetting all its unsteadiness by hearing the mantra, it does not run away anywhere." Because our minds like to "chew" on things, by repeating a *mantra* again and again, it becomes absorbed in it and forgets all other thoughts. The resulting peace is so tangible by its sheer contrast to the restless chatter of the mind, we remember it, especially during moments of duress when we find we can remain remarkably calm.

The repetition of *mantra* is called *japa*, which means "to whisper." There are three stages of *japa* that lead from the gross physical body to our innermost core of silence. First, the *mantra* is repeated out loud according to the rules of Sanskrit pronunciation. (The preferred number of repetitions is 108, the number required to purify all 72,000 nerves in the body.) Next, the *mantra* is repeated silently with just the lips moving and with a faint whisper. Then the *mantra* is pronounced mentally.

The vibrations of the pure sounds purify the yogi's *pancakosha*, or the "five sheaths of the body." The voiced *mantra* purifies the *annamaya kosha*, the layer that's made up of the food we eat. It is also called the "gross physical," or our skin, bones, tissues, organs, and so on. The whispered repetition purifies the *pranamaya kosha*, or the breath that's our life force. And the mental act of *japa* works on the *manomaya kosha* or our "mental body." One of the common obstacles yogis have to achieving silence in meditation is the constant and mundane activity of our thinking mind. But with the mental recitation of *mantra*, our thoughts become absorbed in the feeling of the Sanskrit syllables, stilling the onslaught of mental noise.

When the chatter in our mind ceases, we become aware of a deeper level of intelligence within us, which is the *vijnanamaya kosha* or the subtle intellect. Then the light of pure discrimination dawns. Discrimination allows us to choose that which is most pleasant and uplifting to us. Because the mind finds peace to be the most charming state, it naturally is led to it through the silence following the practice of *mantra*. When we become full of silent peace the mind rests in a natural, content, and happy state, which is the *anandamaya kosha*, or the "bliss-filled body." This is true meditation, the highest form of yoga.

The *mantra*, *Oṁ*, is the best example to explain how the syllables of Sanskrit function to unite body, mind, and breath with the natural cycles of life. The Vedic seers believed that the world begins, sustains, and ends with the three syllables that make up the one sound of *Oṁ*—A, U, and M. The *Mandukya Upanisad* (an ancient yogic text of wisdom) declares that, "AUM stands for the supreme Reality. It is a symbol for what was, what is, and what shall be."

Of all *mantras*, *Oṁ* is the most spiritually charged. It's called a "seed" *mantra* or *bija*, because just like the seed contains the potential for the whole tree, the seed syllable *Om* contains the potential for the whole creation, its maintenance, and its dissolution.

Oṁ is not a symbol, meaning that it points to something outside itself. For example, if we see a nation's flag it is a symbol for the nation. It is not the nation itself. But *Oṁ* itself embodies all the four aspects of creation, maintenance, dissolution, and silence within the sounds that make it up:

> A = Creation, the Navel, the Creator god (Brahma), and the Waking State of Consciousness
>
> U = Maintenance, the Heart and Lungs, the Sustainer god (Visnu), and the Dreaming State of Consciousness
>
> M = Dissolution, The Third Eye, the Transformer god (Siva), and the Deep Sleep State of Consciousness

Sages (and now some scientists) believe *Oṁ* to be the primordial sound that created the universe. Yogis find when you intone "AUM" in your own body you reconnect with the source of creation. Because of its power to generate and rejuvenate life, *Oṁ* is called *pranava* ("life force itself"). But the energizing effects of *Oṁ* are better experienced than described.

Now experience the precise way Oṁ enlivens the energy in your body and connects you to the larger forces of natural law:

Take a deep breath in and exhale by slowly releasing the sound, "aaaaah." If your breath is not shallow, you may notice a sensation in the abdomen. The sound resonates in the same part of the body that is responsible for the creation of another life in women, the womb, and the digestion, which continuously replenishes our bodies with the life-giving nutrients in food throughout our lifetime. In Sanskrit, the vowel sound, "a" corresponds with the function of creation and the waking state of consciousness.

Now take another deep breath in and exhale the sound, "uuuuuh." You may notice a sensation in the upper chest area. This is the location of the heart and lungs, the organs essential to the circulation of blood and nutrients as well as the breath throughout the body. Without the constant beating of the heart and the in and out flow of breath, we would soon find ourselves dead. Like these organs, the Sanskrit vowel, "u" resonates with the maintenance function of the body and the dreaming state of consciousness. Just as the blood and breath pervade the body, when we dream our thoughts pervade the environment.

With a last full breath, release the sound, "mmmm." Feel how it vibrates in the head cavity, directly behind the center of the forehead. This is a very powerful region of the subtle physiology described as the "third eye" or the eye of wisdom.

The final sound of *Oṁ* is the most significant sound in the Sanskrit alphabet. It instills the life force in the *mantra*.

Remember when you were a kid and Mom made something delicious to eat. You would close your eyes and exclaim, "mmmm, good." Also when we come to the end of something, we often feel satisfied. According to Yoga philosophy, creation begins with thought (and sound) and ends in content silence. It is held that the soul enters the body through the top of the head and exits through the same entrance. The uppermost region of the body is associated with dissolution and corresponds with the Sanskrit vowel "m" (also called *anusvara*, or "nasalization") and the state of deep sleep.

Now put all three sounds together. As you breathe out, pronounce "AUM." Feel each of the sounds resonating within the three distinct regions of the body. At the end of several repetitions, simply observe the sensations in the body. You may notice the mind is more silent. This "sound of silence" is said to be the source of creation and the "fourth" state of consciousness, which is peace.

Chapter Seven

The Technology of Sanskrit as Sacred Sound and Modern Science

"Progress of our understanding of physics over the past quarter century has been made by exploring deeper levels of natural law...and what we've discovered at the basis of the universe is this single universal field of intelligence."

~ John Hagelin, Ph.D., Theoretical Physicist

Ringing temple bell, Dunagiri MA Mandir.

As a foreigner studying Sanskrit in Calcutta, I attracted a lot of attention. One member of the press, in particular, was intrigued with my story and asked if he could publish an article in the local newspaper. I obliged.

The article's angle centered around the strangeness of both my and my teacher's circumstance. I'd of course come to India to study Sanskrit. At the same time, my teacher's son had gone to the United States to study physics. The journalist concluded that foreigners are attracted to the old and outdated ways, while Indians are striving for the future.

My teacher, however, didn't see it this way. "Sanskrit *is* physics," he declared. "It perfectly replicates the vibrational code that makes up natural laws. When you learn Sanskrit, you gain access to the structure of the universe itself."

Indeed, the oral transmission of the Vedas in Sanskrit reveals experientially what quantum physics describes as the unified field. From the Vedic perspective not only does it join gravity with light, but the unified field is a *subjectively* intelligent, singular state of Being.

In the Vedic tradition, the basis of creation can only be known by *becoming* it.

This is where science and religion—physics and Veda—cease to bear distinction. And it's where Veda isn't so much about ancient and outdated beliefs, but about providing us with the answers to where modern physics leaves off.

The *rishis* saw and heard in their mind's eye those subtle sounds of Sanskrit become all that's manifest in nature. They documented these strings of code in the form of rhythmic speech, or *mantras*, which make up what are erroneously described as the "hymns" of the Vedas (implying that they are on par with Christian or other devotional songs).

The Vedas are instead the soundtrack of the way the created world arises, mutates and dissolves with respect to the unified field. They are the recordings of what the rishis heard and saw, committed to memory, and passed down through carefully guarded lineages of brahmins who've preserved them orally for centuries.

In this way, the Vedic tradition is a living lineage, allowing a portal to the unified field through Sanskrit.

Veda is also a state of Being that's intelligent. It has self-awareness. It awakens that intelligence within you by being spoken.

When you speak the Vedic mantras precisely according to the rules of Sanskrit and Vedic chanting, they cultivate your subtle nervous system to co-participate with natural law—to function as a channel of universal intelligence. If I require it to rain, for example, by enlivening the string of code in Sanskrit that produces rain with my speech, it *will* rain *(as long as it's dharmically correct to rain).*

According to Vedic tradition, chanting Sanskrit is the key to uncovering the laws of nature. When we chant Sanskrit, we return to the source from where we came. We go to the root. We arrive at the fundamental basis of all animated creation. This is why Sanskrit is not a dead, classical language—but a technology for awakening higher states of consciousness.

The Veda in Sanskrit as a technology that grants access to nature's vibrational code has been kept alive for thousands of generations through *adhyayanam*—the guru-disciple relationship. The teacher awakens the universal intelligence within the student through the constant repetition of Sanskrit.

While yogis have known for centuries the tangible effects of *mantra* on body, mind, and spirit, scientists now corroborate this ancient auditory technology with modern research. The western medical community became aware of the effects of sound on the body with the discoveries made by Dr. Alfred Tomatis, the French medical doctor credited with first observing that fetuses respond to sound stimuli as they develop in the womb.

Serving as the physician for a Benedictine monastery outside of Paris, Dr. Tomatis was called to treat an outbreak of depression among the brothers. After questioning the monks, he learned that the new abbot had recently ended their daily ritual of Gregorian chanting. Dr. Tomatis concluded that without the auditory stimulation of the sacred chants, the monks' central nervous systems regressed into a depressive mode.

After reinstating the practice of group singing, their depression lifted. The results were so immediate that it led Dr. Tomatis to study other forms of sacred chants from world religions. His research culminated in the Tomatis Method, which he claims achieves higher measurements of intelligence through active listening.

Dr. Tomatis' work laid the foundation for the discoveries made by Dr. Susumu Ohno, the chief geneticist of the Beckman Research Institute in Duarte, California. Dr. Ohno ascribed musical notes to each of the six amino acids that make up the DNA. As he transcribed the arrangement of these notes by the DNA helixes in living matter, he observed that the sound patterns are not random, but actually consist of specific melodies. After hearing the melody of a particular type of cancer, Dr. Ohno theorized that its cure might be in realigning the body's melodies to literally a different tune.

And what about the effects of repetition on the brain?

Our Reticular Activating System (RAS) that consists of a bundle of nerve fibers in the medulla oblongata (near the brain stem) is responsible for alerting the brain to the presence of new stimuli. They are the primitive responses we all have to protect us from the threat of danger. The RAS was very useful when we were hunters and gatherers, but in the post-industrial, high tech age we find ourselves bombarded by a continuous assault of noise and images that contribute only to the over-stimulation of our instinctual reactions. Instead of inducing heightened awareness, our brains become dull and unresponsive, inviting disease of both body and mind.

But when a stimulus, such as a *mantra*, becomes repetitive, the RAS grows accustom to it. Ted Melnechuk of the Institute for Advancement of Health claims that when a repetitive sound pattern is pronounced or played in the environment, the brain releases opiate-like endorphins as the RAS relaxes. Instead of inciting the brain to take immediate action, it calms it down instead.

And what about *Oṁ*? Is there any scientific explanation that correlates with that offered by the yogis?

Dr. Ernst Rossi, M.D. suggests in his book, *The Psychobiology of Mind-Body Healing*, that language creates physiological changes in the body. The hypothalamus, located in the mid-lower level of the brain, "communicates" our language via the nerve fibers within the higher cortex to reach the various organs and systems of the body. In this way, the brain sends electrical patterns or brain waves throughout the entire bodily structure that correlate with specific mental and emotional states.

Just as there are three syllables that make up *Oṁ*, brain waves are distinguished according to three types. Beta waves correspond with the waking state and are measured as heightened mental activity, such as we saw with the "*a*" sound of the *mantra*. The "dream state" of the syllable "*u*" mirrors the Alpha waves of the brain in a state of mild relaxation. And the "*m*" syllable that conveys complete satisfaction is experienced in the Theta state of deep relaxation that leads to meditative awareness or higher states of consciousness. Finally Delta brain waves (which scientists associate with dreamless sleep wherein ordinary awareness of "self" is absent) emit the pure silence of the *anahata nada* described by the original yogis. That is the goal of "sonic *samadhi*" gained through the repetition of Sanskrit.

When I first began teaching *Sanskrit for Yogis* to yoga teachers and practitioners, my intention was to inspire their yoga practice toward deeper, transformative experience through sacred sound. What I didn't expect was that anyone would be *healed* from chanting Sanskrit.

Yet I've witnessed students experience remarkable recoveries from central nervous system disorders in particular—such as MS, fibromyalgia, migraine headaches and even stroke—from chanting the Sanskrit alphabet alone. Not only does chanting in Sanskrit lead to the more transcendent mind states that permit the body deep and necessary rest, but pronunciation of the 50 syllables of Sanskrit themselves stimulate the entire *nadi* system of subtle nerve channels in the body with renewed—and healing—*prana*.

Students have also reported relief from depression and anxiety after chanting Sanskrit *mantras*. One student (who is a pain management physician) plays recordings of Sanskrit *mantras* in her office when she meets patients and she's said they've all remarked at how calm and peaceful they felt in an otherwise stressful environment. She's even begun to prescribe *mantras* for anxiety and pain, recognizing the powerful effects sacred sound has on establishing harmony in the body and mind.

It's said that the future of medicine is vibrational healing. We've only touched the tip of the iceberg that Sanskrit represents as an important contribution to the advancement of this knowledge. It's a veritable ocean of wisdom—that's both scientific and sacred.

Baba Dhanvantari Giri (Master Healer and Yogi), Dunagiri.

Author at the Vaishnavi Devi Temple, Dunagiri, India.

Conclusion

Sanskrit, The Next Step on Your Yoga Journey

"Chanting in Sanskrit is pure ambrosia, a sublime experience of precious vibration which gives profound inner peace. It is a song of praise to the divinity dwelling in the heart. It dispels illnesses and gives robust health, increases knowledge, strength, and fame, leading one to the realization of the Self of all."

~ Swami Brahmananda Sarasvati

Sadhu on pilgrimage, Chardham, 2010.

Sanskrit chanting has been part of my daily practice now for over 20 years. It's not only been a powerful tool for unlocking the limitless reserves of energy within, it's been a constant companion that's both helped and uplifted me during all the moments of my life.

I've chanted when I've been happy and content—as well as when tears rained down. I've chanted when my throat's been choked with grief so strong I could barely muster the *mantras*. And yet I've chanted in joy and celebration with far greater ease. I've chanted on the death beds of those whose passing seemed imminent, but after hearing these divine *mantras* received a "second wind."

I've chanted on mountain tops and in deserts, in temples and in graveyards, while facing exquisite oceans and while spending the night in sterile, lonely—and sometimes icky—hotel rooms. I've chanted to center my mind while waiting for flights in busy airports. I've chanted quietly to myself on long hauls across the seas back and forth to India.

I've chanted when I can't figure out what's best to do, yet the solution always comes at the end, in the silence.

Chanting in Sanskrit is to yoga what breath is to the body, and in fact both are the same. Sanskrit is your life-enhancer that's as easy to access as making a sound. It puts you in touch with that part of you that's whole, always has been whole and always will be whole.

Sanskrit is not something one struggles to learn but uses to remember who you are and where you came from. If the world was spoken into being, Sanskrit is the echo. Because it's echoing in all things, you can hear it and repeat it and return to your source.

Sanskrit in this way is a *sadhana*, a practice of remembrance. It's also as healing and beneficial as its complimentary *sadhanas—asana, pranayama* and meditation. Most of all, it's easy. If you can make a sound, you can chant in Sanskrit. You don't need special musical skills—just a willingness to make the sound correctly and feel its feeling within you.

Now that you know the power of Sanskrit as a technology for awakening and expanding your consciousness, it's time to take the next step and experience it for yourself. For this aim, I've created a series of learning products to assist you in easily attaining the beautiful and transforming goal of yoga. These are not just classes where you learn some information. It's an opportunity for a profound experience to enliven your inner light.

For centuries, learning to chant Sanskrit and feel its primordial sounds have been at the basis of the Vedic, Yoga, and Tantra traditions. That's because of Sanskrit's power to tone and strengthen the subtle nervous system, making the body, mind and spirit fit for the higher stages of Yoga.

Yet there's a mistaken notion among Yogis that Sanskrit is a dead, classical language that you think you probably should know something about but feel like it involves some kind of long and painful commitment to learn it.

That's what I thought over 20 years ago, which is why I enrolled in graduate school to study it in the academic way.

And truthfully?

I'd spend hours at a desk surrounded by tall books of grammar, pencil filings, erasure dust, and a pile of the hair I pulled out of my head trying to decode this incredibly intricate and complex language.

It wasn't until I sat with traditional teachers of Sanskrit in Nepal and India that I realized there's a much more joyful and spiritually enlightened approach to derive the full-blown experience of Sanskrit as the actual vibration of your soul-filled consciousness—the same consciousness that allows you to read the words on this page as well as comprehend the intricate workings of the universe both seen and unseen.

This is why Sanskrit is the language of the *devas*, the universal principles of light that form the complete laws of nature. And it's the language of Yoga because its 50 distinct sounds enliven and awaken your inner core—uniting body, breath, and spirit.

In the past, you had to be born into a family of Brahmin priests to experience this profound technology of higher consciousness, which is why few Yogis in the West have access to Sanskrit as it's traditionally used in the practice of Yoga and meditation in India. But now through the blessings of my revered teachers, you can derive the same benefits of sacred sound to bring more joy, light, and consciousness to your Yoga and meditation practice.

Learning Sanskrit authentically requires the physical transmission of a living teacher. Yet in these times, it's not always possible to sit with a teacher in person. Fortunately, our virtual environments are becoming more real in that you can derive great benefits through online learning in lieu of opportunities for live interactions.

To assist you in your learning, I've created a virtual immersion in traditional Vedic Sanskrit: *Sanskrit for Yogis, An Introduction to Nada, the Yoga of Sacred Sound.* At the heart of this online program is the same experience of *adhyayanam* (guru-disciple method) that forms the basis of Vedic transmission. Through listening and repeating you'll gain access to the power of Sanskrit chanting for healing and advancing your yoga and meditation practice.

You'll learn the precise pronunciation of the 50 Sanskrit syllables and how to recite them as a *sadhana* or spiritual practice. You'll discover how Sanskrit *mantra* is best used as a tool for meditation. You'll be introduced to chanting the Vedas in Sanskrit according to the six rules of Vedic chanting. You'll experience how Sanskrit stimulates and awakens the subtle nervous system, specifically the seven energy centers, the *cakras*. And finally, you'll learn how to read the beginning *devanagari* Sanskrit characters.

With a solid foundation in the basics of Vedic Sanskrit, I invite you to participate in my more advanced programs or continue on where your journey takes you. My goal is to inspire you toward deeper experience of the enlightening power of Sanskrit as it's been preserved and transmitted throughout ages of time in India. And I wish to give you an opportunity to evolve your yoga practice from the physical performance of postures to a more rarefied experience of your own transcendental light.

The experience of awakening with Sanskrit is a limitless ocean. Come dive in!

Lokah Samastah Sukhino Bhavantu!
May All Beings Be Happy!
Dr. Katy Jane

Dr. Katy with elderly pilgrim, Haridwar, 2010.

Drops in the Ocean:

Student Experiences of Sanskrit

"You are not a drop in the ocean, you are the entire ocean in a drop."

~ Rumi

I often mused about my teacher's prediction that I'd one day teach women specifically to chant Sanskrit. He described them as "oceans of ladies." I had no idea what that meant. I wasn't learning Sanskrit to teach it. I really loved being a student. I still do.

Yet as the years progressed in the *Sanskrit for Yogis* project, I noticed a certain profile of student who was attracted to this *sadhana*. My classes were (and still are) predominantly attended by women. And not just any kind of woman. A new woman. A woman with a voice. A woman who awakens to her power through her voice. A woman committed to waking up. And she's sensitive enough to recognize Sanskrit—the power of speech—as one of her inherent *shaktis* (feminine empowerments) given to women as living goddesses.

Yet it wasn't long ago in India's past when women weren't even permitted to hear the Vedas, let alone chant them. In my own lifetime, I once attended a Vedic *yajna* (fire offering) in a small town in the American Midwest wherein women were expected to sit behind a curtain while male priests performed the ceremony, fearing their menstruating bodies might contaminate its holiness.

It's revolutionary that women around the world are chanting the Vedas in Sanskrit irrespective of their religion or culture—and deriving great benefit and awakening from doing so. Women are occupying voices of power.

Women attending Sacred Sadhana Immersion, Dunagiri Retreat, 2019.

To honor the voices I've been fortunate to inspire with my *Sanskrit for Yogis* project, I now devote the remaining pages of this little book on awakening with Sanskrit, to these "oceans of ladies." When I first got the idea to offer this traditional approach to learning Sanskrit, I had no idea the kind of impact it would make on women's lives. It's said that if you awaken one woman, the entire community awakens. It's happening the world over. The goddess is rising.

This is the latest chapter in the book of Vedas, which are timeless and unending. And yet it has yet to be written. And these pioneers are its authors.

Margo's Story

I became highly motivated to learn Sanskrit when my dear friend Suzi Worthington was diagnosed with stage IV colon cancer. After surgery and chemotherapy, Suzi and I spent quality time together diving into craniosacral therapies and yoga practices to help her recovery. As we worked together, the desire to go deeper into Patanjali's *Yoga Sutras* kept arising.

It has been said by the sages, "when you ask, the teacher appears" and like magic, within days of quietly asking for a *sutras* mentor, we were introduced to the teachings of Dr. Katy Jane through her long time student, Shelley Christopherson. Rather than analyze the *sutras*, Shelley recommended we chant them.

Immediately we felt the effects of chanting as powerful medicine. Each time we chanted together a feeling of wholeness, peace, and deep connection would manifest. Katy beautifully describes this process of attuning with nature and with the whole universe through the technology of Sanskrit in her online course, *Sanskrit for Yogis*. In this course we further immersed ourselves in the Sanskrit alphabet and Vedic invocations. We were hooked! Chanting became a way we could access a vibration that led to peace of body, mind and spirit despite the stress, trauma and relentlessness of cancer. Several months prior to establishing our chanting group, Suzi had been to India for a glorious six weeks of Ayurveda treatments. While there, her Indian practitioners encouraged daily chanting to be part of her treatment plan. Now we had the tools to do so!

Sanskrit chanting became a priority, a sweet way for us to spend quality time together. We enjoyed simply BEING with one another in this purely absorbed state without the hindrance of body or mind. We cultivated this vibrational nectar together throughout the rest of Suzi's cancer journey. Death wasn't something we spoke much about. Suzi's mental focus was on living. Nevertheless at the end, chanting helped her transition over to the next phase of her spiritual journey. She left her earthly body with the voices of her loved ones in her ears.

Right after Suzi's death, Shelley and I helped soothe our aching hearts and the hearts of our devastated community by chanting the *Mahamrityunjaya Mantra* 108 times. The vibration of the mantra took over our bodies, hearts and minds, morphing Suzi's spirit and her loved ones together in deep connection. We chant for Suzi each year on the anniversary of her passing.

"Not only has Sanskrit chanting strengthened my relationships with others but it has profoundly enhanced my personal meditation and spiritual practices."

Not only has Sanskrit chanting strengthened my relationships with others but it has profoundly enhanced my personal meditation and spiritual practices. I became interested in meditation after reading Eknath Easwaran's brilliant book, *Passage Meditation*, many years ago. His beautiful and poignant perspective on the benefits of meditation motivated me to dedicate to a daily practice. Although I felt the benefits of the practice for the rest of my day, the time actually spent in meditation was difficult, challenging and often felt like a chore. After learning the art of Vedic Invocation, meditation has become a source of deep joy, a celebration of being alive in the present moment and fully inhabiting my body as an instrument in perfect tune with itself.

My professional life has also blossomed with my chanting life. The summer before Suzi's passing, I was approached to teach yoga classes at a local cancer center. Without hesitation I said, "Yes!" Creating a yoga program for cancer patients, survivors and their care givers has been a way to integrate all my favorite yoga therapies; yoga nidra, Sanskrit chanting, gentle *asana* and metta mediation. In addition to being the Adjunct Instructor of Yoga for the University of Alaska Anchorage, I am now co-owner of *Yoga Therapists of Alaska, LLC* with my soul sister, Shelley Christopherson. We are dedicated to teaching and training the next generation of yoga teachers to integrate Sanskrit into their yoga tool box.

Life is rich and using the sacred technology of *Nada Yoga* has magnified its riches.

Margo Sorum, *E-RYT, C-IAYT, YACEP*
Yoga Therapists of Alaska, LLC

Mindy's Story

I have been a student of yoga for over 20 years and teaching for 18 of those. The wealth of wisdom that we call yoga continues to astonish me. Yoga is so much more than just the asana, or postures that most Westerners think of. Yoga is a rich fabric of many colors and layers and it is almost impossible to honor it fully without some knowledge of its origins and its language.

Sanskrit has been a big part of my yogic journey. While I am no Sanskrit scholar, studying with Katy through *Sanskrit for Yogis* has given me a level of understanding of this multifaceted language that I have yet to find anywhere else. Chanting in Sanskrit connects me to this ancient lineage of yoga and the people who have practiced these same mantras through millennia. It gives me a depth of experience that just isn't possible with English translations.

Sanskrit is so simple and so complex all at the same time. In so many ways it reflects the life we lead here on Earth. It can be a tool that keeps us limited in the mind, studying so hard to get all the technical aspects of this language just right. Or it can set us free by feeling it in our hearts, our bodies and moving beyond our limited minds. I love to tap into Sanskrit in a way that I can relate to and that is how Katy teaches her students. Feel this language in you. You already know it. Using it wakes up a dormant part of you that is just waiting for the right conditions to be aroused. You are more than you are aware of and Sanskrit is one tool we can use to tap into some of your limitless potential.

One of the most profound examples of the power of Sanskrit in my life was while

I was pregnant with my first daughter. I chose to do my first large devotional *mantra* practice and dedicate it to my daughter's spiritual development while she was growing in my womb. "Oṁ Namo Bhagavate Vasudevaya" is said to have this effect on babies. I knew she would develop well physically because I trusted in the wisdom of my body. I wanted to devote time and energy to her spiritual wellbeing with 10,000 repetitions of this mantra.

Sanskrit is the key to understanding how we are all connected through vibration."

I'd love to tell you how easy it was to chant 10,000 repetitions. But, I can't. I made progress but was inconsistent with the practice for most of the pregnancy. Eventually, around the 8th month I decided to get serious with it. I chanted every day at least one *mala* of the *mantra* and put my whole heart into the practice. The most miraculous part was that the day after I finished my 10,000th repetition she was born! Two weeks early at that! She was simply waiting for me to get my act together and finish the devotion to her.

In many ways, Katy has been an inspiration to me and to my path of yoga. I am so grateful that she ignited the passion I have for Sanskrit and the richness it has brought to my life. Who would have guessed that a country hippy girl who grew up in Nebraska would end up geeking out on this vibrational language?! It all comes down to that – vibration. And Sanskrit is the key to understanding how we are all connected through vibration.

Mindy Arbuckle
Founder of Maitri Yoga
Author of *7 Steps to Happy*

Shelley's Story

Sanskrit transformed my life.

When I met Katy Jane, I was at the climax of my yoga *asana* journey. I was young, fit, and obsessed with all thing's 'yoga'. However, there was a call for something deeper. I had enough awareness and education to sense that what westerners were practicing as 'yoga' was just skimming the surface. I knew that there was another avenue, and that chanting Sanskrit was integral to making the journey. However, I did have some obstacles: I lived in a small rural town in Alaska, with very little internet service, and no Sanskrit teachers within a 2,000-mile radius. When I discovered Katy and her distance learning programs, I diligently dove in with her prerecorded CD's.

> "When my mind would be overwhelmed by anxiety, fear and doubt; Sanskrit chanting became a way to manage my mental health."

With the practice, I began to notice really interesting effects. One being that after chanting, I felt as if I had just taken a 2-hour yoga class: calm, serene, and enlivened. I began to sleep better, meditate easier, and make healthier choices for my body.

That is when I knew something special was going on. Katy's distinct methodology that she designed for yoga practitioners threw a bright, nurturing light into my life. What I considered 'yoga practice' radically transformed. Using my own voice, and exploring the feeling in the body using the 50 sounds of the Sanskrit alphabet, became the most succinct way to gain access to the meditative state.

Every time my daily life swung out of balance, I found myself using Sanskrit chanting to re-center, reconnect, and establish myself in the present moment. When my mind would be overwhelmed by anxiety, fear and doubt; Sanskrit chanting became a way to manage my mental health. When I broke my leg and needed surgery; Sanskrit chanting became a way to practice yoga when I could not do *asana*. When I was lonely, isolated and depressed working in a corporate environment; Sanskrit chanting became a way to connect with other like-minded individuals.

There are a multitude of these scenarios that have arisen over the past 12 years. Throughout it all, Sanskrit chanting has been the constant companion. The tool that I keep returning to. The technology that works on a number of levels within my being. It is my antidote, my refuge, and the greatest gift I have ever received.

After many years of cultivating a friendship with Katy, I now feel honored to receive her blessing to teach her methodology. Teaching Sanskrit chanting has brought so much joy, community, and meaning into my life and career. It has become the focal point of this life's journey. I look forward to collaborating with Katy, and for the opportunity to cultivate a passion for Sanskrit chanting in others.

Shelley Christopherson, *C-IAYT, E-RYT*
Owner of Yoga Therapists of Alaska, LLC

Francesca's Story

My favorite book when I was a little girl was a big book with lots of pictures, published by *Life*. It was called *The Five Great Religions of the World*. I read the word *Veda* for the first time in the Hinduism chapter. I really had no grasp of what it meant—I was 7 years old at the time.

As a young adult, I learned formal mantra meditation. Maharishi Mahesh Yogi, who brought Eastern meditation to the West, often talked about the importance of being able to read the Veda yourself. The only way to do that was by learning Sanskrit.

Years later, I wandered in and out of a couple different Sanskrit programs that were in existence, before I walked into *Sanskrit for Yogis*. I found them 'dry' and 'rote'; the language itself was not 'alive' the way it was being taught. It wasn't until Katy invited me to study Sanskrit as part of a small group - predominantly women - in a living room in Boulder, that Sanskrit became alive for me. Correct pronunciation of the alphabet was emphasized at the same time we were learning actual Vedic chanting.

The magic appeared with the first chant we learned—the *Shiva Manasa Puja*. Our group was invited to a yoga studio to chant as part of their Shivaratri celebration. After the formal celebration, we went back to the house and completed 108 repetitions of the verses. I remember driving home from Boulder to Denver, and being higher than a kite—literally. It was the first time that I fully understood, through direct experience, the power of the Sanskrit alphabet as *mantra*, and the impact it has on all aspects of one's being. I was committed to going deeper.

In the early years of studying *Sanskrit for Yogis*, I was traveling a lot—almost weekly—teaching meditation and *pranayama* in different venues. I would devour the lessons on the plane and write out the whole lesson word-for-word into my notebook. I would then transfer everything into a 'special' book that became my touchstone for learning. Every word became like a precious jewel, and I found that practically everything Katy said was applied knowledge that led to a deeper understanding.

"The magic appeared with the first chant we learned - the *Shiva Manasa Puja*."

Katy taught us about *likhita shastra*—the writing of texts —and the powerful effect it holds. This became—and still is—my 'go to' practice. I started transliterating texts from *devanagari* to English alphabet, using IAST (International Alphabet of Sanskrit Transliteration). It was commitment to this as a practice that led me to the ability to read *devanagari* script. The process of transliterating and repetitive chanting from that, seems to instill the meaning of the text on a subconscious level. It has become an essential part of my life. I give complete credit to the way I learned from my *Sanskrit for Yogis* classes.

In my early days of learning on my own, I transliterated a chant called the *Chamakam*. It is about asking the Divine for varied things. After I had chanted it twice daily a number of days in a row, I realized that all of a sudden, it began to feel easy and comfortable for me to ask for things in my own life—something that had not previously been a skill that I had.

Rarely a week goes by that I'm not doing something related to Sanskrit. Transliterating texts from *devanagari* is my favorite, because it puts me in a calm, meditative state—no matter how I start out.

Francesca A. Jackson, *DC*

Laurie's Story

I was first exposed to Sanskrit through my meditation teacher Odin Oftedal in 1992. Once I got over the initial fear of the unknown of what it meant to chant, the seed of my curiosity of Sanskrit's meaning and purpose was planted. Over time with a very small Satsang and personal practice, I began incidentally experiencing the calming effects of very simple chanting. My wonder grew, yet there were so many questions unanswered. Then in 2008, I was ecstatic when I heard *Sanskrit for Yogis* with Dr. Katy was going to be hosted in Alaska by Lynne Minton.

Sanskrit for Yogis with Dr. Katy gave a depth and breadth of Sanskrit beyond my dreams. Dr. Katy sets the foundation of the historical intent and practices of Sanskrit. She graciously offers the studies in such a nature as to provide answers that are applicable to aspects of our whole being and daily life. Through sharing historical applications and writings, Sanskrit is shown to have use beyond exploring esoteric topics. The intellect of the mind is explored such that Sanskrit can be used to shape the mind in practical ways - not only through understanding of translation and the meaning conveyed, but ultimately through the experience of Sanskrit chanting. She addresses the science of the mind and anatomy of the body's response to the practices. Dr. Katy translates Sanskrit to a granular level that exposes the underlying interconnection of meaning within the language.

Most importantly, though, is that Dr. Katy teaches in such a manner that one can begin to experience the effects of the science and technology that Sanskrit truly has to offer in one's own body and being. This happens with her expertise in teaching of even the simplest, basic sounds found in nature. Ultimately, Dr. Katy teaches to all aspects of the human being. The mind can then indeed let go to dive deep into the full experience of consciousness.

My practice of Sanskrit chanting cultivates an auspicious mindset and momentum in a direction of optimal wellness. Sanskrit chanting is a focal point for my daily practices. The practice provides a reference point to continually return to and a refuge during life's challenges and joys. These practices affect me on a mental, emotional, physical, and spiritual level to gain access to and

Dr. Katy teaches in such a manner that one can begin to experience the effects of the science and technology that Sanskrit truly has to offer in one's own body and being.

continually return to what I know to be my true nature. The study of the ancient practice's translation with Dr. Katy continues to amaze me as its truths are confirmed to be in alignment with the latest findings in western medicine and mind-body science.

I am extremely grateful for the privilege of studying with Dr. Katy. Her passion and depth of understanding of Sanskrit is contagious. What is even more amazing is her ability to communicate the fullness of her true love of Sanskrit in an accessible and practical manner. The practices of Sanskrit are practical and integral to my daily life as I continue my life's journey. Daily Sanskrit practices ground me in what is truly valuable in my life – clarity of perspective, love, presence, and service.

Laurie Schaeffer, *RN*

Candace's Story

I was first introduced to Dr. Katy and Sanskrit during my yoga teacher training in 2007. I knew that Sanskrit was part of the yogic tradition, but I didn't know why or how it fit in. I was also very intimidated by it. I heard one of the ladies that ran the yoga studio chant a quick invocation after class one day, and I thought she must be some amazing being to know how to do that! I didn't think it was something I could ever learn to do.

I was not in the best place emotionally or spiritually at this time. My husband and I had been married for 3 years and bought a nice large house to start a family in. Little did we know, that wouldn't be happening for us. I had graduated college and left my job, planning to be a stay at home mom for a while. But once I found out that my infertility could not be remedied by medical intervention, I had to figure out what to do next. So I decided to expand my practice of yoga into teaching.

I was so excited to become one of those seemingly magical yoga teachers, with the soothing voice and the ability to use secret knowledge to help transform the people in class from an anxious state to one of peaceful calm. At least that's how I felt after taking a yoga class and I wanted to be able to pass that on. But as my training progressed, I realized there wasn't much special about it and the trainers knew little more than I had already learned in my own studies. That was until Sanskrit day came up on our syllabus.

I remember wanting to stay home that day. What could they possibly teach about Sanskrit in one afternoon, anyway? I didn't realize we were having guest teacher, Dr. Katy, so I was intrigued once I got there and found out we were waiting for her to arrive. I sat in the back, as I usually do, because I like to observe from a distance before I engage.

When Dr. Katy arrived, she had us rearrange into a big circle on the floor. There went my quiet observation plan. I hoped she wasn't going to try to make us chant on the first day! But she did. Only the way she did it made it easy. It wasn't intimidating or confusing. It was fun and exciting. Her explanation of the technology of Sanskrit made so much sense. Why had I never heard this before? And how could she make this "dead language" so fascinating and actually useful in modern life? I decided I had to find out more.

At the end of class I purchased one of Dr. Katy's learning CDs she had brought with her. I mastered my first few short invocations that way, even without learning the alphabet. She'd make the sounds, I'd repeat them, then she'd string them together as she went on with the recorded lesson. I have always been sensitive to energy, especially the fluctuations in my own energy. I could feel something shifting within me. Each time I'd chant, my mind felt clearer and brighter. I was more alert and intentional with my days. I became a better decision maker and I could simply tolerate life without feeling like it gut-punched me every day. I'd either feel calm and relaxed, or an excited buzz that urged me on throughout the day and helped me engage with the things I needed and wanted to do.

I should probably mention that I had been a pretty stressed out child. I'd get debilitating migraines from the stress, and as I got older, it turned into a generalized anxiety. There were several times in my teens and early twenties I'd just leave a job or decide not to do something important, because I didn't know how it would turn out and the scenarios that ran through my mind were intolerable. I was ambitious, but would get too cautious or nervous to follow my ambitions through to completion. Then one day, only about three months after I started chanting, I realized that was no longer the case.

In fact, I had made plans to open my own yoga studio. This was something I never would have entertained before. Way too many stressful things to consider! Too much could go wrong. Plus, I was a newly certified teacher. I did it anyway and it went pretty well! I also learned a lot more Sanskrit. I took Dr. Katy's Sanskrit and Yoga Mastery course and then her Jyotisha certification course. Soon I could easily learn to chant things like the Yoga Sutras and the Bhagavad Gita. When I say "easily learn," I'm not exaggerating. She made it so easy.

The ironic thing is that all of this led me to what I really wanted. A family.

"There are millions of yoga practitioners, but I have come across very few who know about Sanskrit beyond the fact that the names of the poses are in Sanskrit."

That sounds strange, I know. It was a complete impossibility for me to have biological children. At that time, I knew a private adoption wasn't right. It was very expensive and my research into it turned me off, when I realized we'd basically have to advertise ourselves to birth mothers and wait to get chosen. Not that there is anything wrong with that, but it didn't feel like the right way for us to find our children. I still wanted babies but had no idea how it could be possible. It wasn't until Dr. Katy read my birth chart that it became clear. How had I never thought of it myself? I have no idea. It was foster care. There is a star in my birth chart that indicates I could be a foster mother.

That story is long and twisty and involved. But the way it relates to Sanskrit is no small thing. Sanskrit, in my experience, cured my anxiety. Not only did it cure my anxiety, but it helped me be more assertive in my speech and actions. So when I got my first call about a baby in the NICU and was told I'd be meeting the birth parents before taking him home, I didn't want to say "no way," because it was new and scary territory. I wanted to go get my son. I knew he was ours from day one. I've had a lot of that "knowing" in so many areas of life, since I began to chant all those years ago.

When I'd have to go to court and speak to the judge about how the kids in our care were doing, or talk to their attorneys and caseworkers when they'd come to evaluate our home and the children, I didn't feel intimidated like I would have before. There is no way I could've handled that intense nine-year experience without the help of Sanskrit (and a little Jyotisha, too.) In the end, we have four amazing forever children, and were privileged to help several others along the way as well.

You'll hear Dr. Katy talk about aligning with your highest life's purpose. There are many ways to get there. For some people it could take years of therapy, self-help books, life coaches, or plain hard life lessons. For me, the fastest, easiest, and most surprising way, was learning to chant. It cleared the confusion in my mind and my emotional body. It aligned me with higher universal truths, and it helped me see how much I was capable of. It has been there for me in times I needed to reduce the stress I felt building inside or to fall asleep when my mind was racing. It has even helped my kids through some tough emotional times when I'd chant over them, and now that they are a little older, with them. I could go on, but it would take a whole book.

When you hear that Sanskrit is a technology for awakening, believe it. It is a gift for those who are lucky enough to be exposed to it. Perhaps it isn't luck. I think Sanskrit finds you. There are millions of yoga practitioners, but I have come across very few who know about Sanskrit beyond the fact that the names of the poses are in Sanskrit. I read in an obscure book a while back, that there would come a time when this ancient technology would be revealed to more and more people. That there would be a few teachers coming forth, teaching Sanskrit to help change the consciousness of the world. Dr. Katy is definitely one of those people and I feel so fortunate to have been part of this bigger, what I believe will be significant and historical, awakening experience.

Candace Kirchner
Realtor and mother of four

Sanskrit for Yogis immersion, Samadhi Center for Yoga, Denver, 2006.

Glossary

"Like the word and its meaning united,
For the right understanding of word and meaning,
I venerate the two parents of the universe,
Parvata and the supreme lord, Shiva."
~ Kalidasa

Priest chanting Vedas, Dunagiri MA temple.

Abhinavagupta	Prolific *guru* of Kashmir Shaiva lineage (born 950 CE) famous for his composition of *Tantraloka* (12 volumes) and his deep insights on Sanskrit poetics, mysticism, philosophy, aesthetics, and phonematic emanation (theories on the expansion of sound).
Adi Shankara	Founder of Shankaracharya lineage of Advaita Vedanta (non-dualism); famed for his enlightened commentaries on the *Bhagavad Gita*, the *Brahma Sutras*, and also for his beautiful musical and poetic compositions such as *Shiva Manasa Puja, Lahiri Sundari, Dakshinamurti Stotram,* among others.
anandamaya kosha	The bliss-filled sheath, covering, or layer of the subtle human body.
asana	Presence, existence, one's silent abode, a quiet seat; anything that is done without interruption and with full attention, posture; the *Hatha Yoga Pradipika* lists 84 postures of the Yoga system, five of which are the most important: *padmasana, bhadrasana, vajrasana, virasana, svastikasana.*
bija	Seed, element, primary cause or principle; the source or origin of something; the true, underlying cause of anything coming into being.

bindu — A detached particle or drop; the dot over a letter representing the *anusvara* (nasalization); sudden expression like a drop of oil in water expanding; the appearance of the universe from a sudden big bang; a tiny, concentrated drop of life; the center of any *yantra* (meditation diagram); the third eye center.

brahmana (Brahmin) — One who has divine knowledge; a priest; the name for a class of Vedic scriptures that contain rules for the use of *mantras* (where, when, by whom, and to which deity) and detailed explanations of their origins and meanings.

cakra — Circle making, a potter's wheel, a circle or sphere, a cycle of years or seasons; the winding of a river, a whirlpool, an energetic sphere in the subtle body.

candra bindu — A Moon drop, the archaic Vedic form of the *anusvara* that is contained within the *devanagari* syllable *Oṁ* (ॐ).

deva — Heavenly, shining; light-filled being; a deity, a god; a force responsible for a particular law of nature; one who sports or plays.

devanagari — *Devanagari*, meaning "divine" (*deva*) and "city" (*nagari*), refers to one of the systems used to write down the oral Sanskrit syllables. The word, *devanagari*, translates as "city of the gods," or more loosely, "the container of divine light." The script most commonly used to depict Sanskrit characters, the outer symbols that express the intercommunication between human and divine.

devi — A female light-filled being; a goddess; an emissary of *shakti*; the feminine principle activating the creative processes of life.

guru — Heavy, weighty, difficult to digest, great, large, excessive, difficult, hard; a venerable and respected person, a teacher of the highest knowledge, a real "heavy dude."

mantra — An instrument of thought, a potent prayer or string of Sanskrit syllables having the power to transform, enliven, and purify the body and environment; a sacred Sanskrit verse that makes up the sound form of a deity or law of nature; the inner or secret design of creation in the form of unfolding sound patterns.

marma The Sanskrit word for *marma* means "mortal" or "vulnerable point" referring to tender, weak or sensitive access points located anatomically at sites where veins, arteries, tendons, bones or joints intersect. Localized vital energy points on the surface of the body that are infused with *prana* and imbued with consciousness, serving as acupoint bridges or doorways between the body, mind and soul. Affect the flow and balance of *prana* when stimulated to aid healing of vital organs.

nada The sound of the vibration of the universe; the resounding echo of creation; the unfolding melody of existence.

nataraja The lord of the dance, a name for *Shiva* who creates the world through the resonation of his thunderous *tandava* (foot stomps); the motion of his dance articulates the shape of a cosmic *Oṁ* that activates the divine cycles of creation, maintenance, and destruction.

pandita (Panditji) Learned, wise, skilled in something; a scholar, teacher or one who speaks about sacred things and subjects with divine authority.

prana	The breath of life, living spirit, total vitality within and without.
pranamaya kosha	One of the five sheaths or coverings surrounding the subtle body made up of vital life breath.
pranava	A name describing the *mantra Om*, meaning primordial sound that is the source of all life-force.
pranayama	The restraint or control of the life force (*prana*) in the body through the practice of measuring and conscious direction of the breath; the fourth limb of the eightfold yoga practice according to Patanjali.
rishi	A seer (and hearer) of the divine impulses of intelligence emanating from the source of creation; a singer of sacred hymns; a poet or sage; any person who alone or with others invokes the deities of nature using rhythmical Sanskrit speech; an awakened one who sees, hears, and repeats the Truth.

samadhi — Putting together, joining or combining, a union, a whole, an aggregate; completion, accomplishment, bringing into harmony; profound meditation; a kind of trance or suspension of ordinary consciousness; the eighth limb of the yoga path according to Patanjali; a sanctuary or tomb of a saint.

samskrita — Put together, constructed, well or completely formed; perfected, purified, consecrated, sanctified, hallowed, initiated, refined, adorned, ornamented, polished; the perfected language of pure consciousness.

shakti — Power, strength, might, ability, energy; the energy or active power of a deity personified as a divine feminine principle; the primal creative power; the great goddess who activates and causes the final dissolution of all life.

shiva — Auspicious, propitious, gracious, favorable; benign, kind, benevolent; the deity responsible for dissolution, destruction, transcendence and also creation.

shruti That which was heard; a name for the Vedas that were divinely cognized by the ancient *rishis*; a stream, flow, or effusion of the melodious pure vibrations of consciousness that allow it to become manifest in creation.

sutra Little thread, a sacred thread, a thread running through cloth holding it together; refers to the verses of a sacred work as in the Yoga Sutras, the smallest form of expression that only contains the most necessary words. They are called little threads based on the belief that it only takes a small thread of knowledge to save a person drowning in ignorance. Krishna said to Arjuna in the *Bhagavad Gita, "Even a small bit of this knowledge saves one from great fear and suffering."*

upanisad The sitting down at the feet of another to listen to her words; secret knowledge given in this manner, the mystery that underlies or rests underneath the external system of things, "secret doctrine"; a class of philosophical writings whose aim is the exposition of the secret meaning of the Vedas.

veda	Wisdom; true or sacred knowledge pertaining to the source, cause, and purpose of life; a collection of four divisions of knowledge: *Rig* (creation), *Yajur* (ritual maintenance of human life), *Sama* (celestial melodies of creation), *Atharva* (fire and Soma offerings to the ancestors); each of the Vedas has two distinct parts, *mantra* and *brahmana*. Together the *mantras* and *brahmanas* of the Vedas form the complete cognition of pure consciousness heard and seen by the *rishis*.
vijnanamaya kosha	One of five sheaths covering the subtle body made up of the intellect that regulates discrimination and wisdom.
yantra	An instrument either flat or three-dimensional composed of geometrical arrangements together with Sanskrit *mantras* used to induce meditation through the visual sense.

Katy Jane, Ph.D First Edition Printing: August 2019

To learn more about our upcoming *Sanskrit for Yogis immersions,* please visit:

- www.DrKatyJane.com
- info@DrKatyJane.com
- namaste@drkatyjane.com

Printed in Great Britain
by Amazon

55165568R00075